Praise for

quantum CREATIVITY

*"A new view of consciousness is arising, in which consciousness
is infinite, eternal, and one. This new view has radical implications for
the creative process, as physicist Amit Goswami shows in his splendid
book, **Quantum Creativity**. In the new view, the solitary individual gives
way to collective wisdom spanning past, present, and future. Thus the
source of creativity and the fount of wisdom are potentially infinite.
Goswami has painted a majestic picture of what it means to
be human, on which our future may depend."*

—Larry Dossey, M.D., author of *One Mind: How Our Individual
Mind Is Part of a Greater Consciousness and Why It Matters*

*"Amit Goswami writes with as much wisdom, intelligence, humor,
and spiritual insight as his Bengali forefathers—great minds like physicist
Jagadish Chandra Bose, poet Rabindranath Tagore, and mystic Swami
Vivekananda. Goswami's move from quantum physicist to motivational
and spiritual teacher/writer takes considerable daring."*

—Fred Alan Wolf, a.k.a. Dr. Quantum, author of *Time Loops and
Space Twists: How God Created the Universe*

quantum
CREATIVITY

ALSO BY AMIT GOSWAMI, PH.D.

The Self-Aware Universe

God Is Not Dead

The Quantum Doctor

Physics of the Soul

The Visionary Window

Creative Evolution

How Quantum Activism Can Save Civilization

quantum
CREATIVITY

Think Quantum, Be Creative

Amit Goswami, Ph.D.

HAY HOUSE, INC.
Carlsbad, California • New York City
London • Sydney • New Delhi

Published in the United States by: Hay House, Inc.: www.hayhouse.com® • *Published in Australia by:* Hay House Australia Pty. Ltd.: www.hayhouse.com.au • *Published in the United Kingdom by:* Hay House UK, Ltd.: www.hayhouse.co.uk • *Published in India by:* Hay House Publishers India: www.hayhouse.co.in

Indexer: Jay Kreider
Cover design: Angela Moody • *Interior design:* Pamela Homan

Sydney Harris Cartoon printed by permission of Sydney Harris © ScienceCartoons Plus.com
Guernica © 2013 Estate of Pablo Picasso / Artists Rights Society (ARS), New York
M.C. Escher's "Drawing Hands" © 2013 The M.C. Escher Company-The Netherlands. All rights reserved. www.mcescher.com
"On Beauty" from THE PROPHET by Kahlil Gibran, copyright © 1923 by Kahlil Gibran and renewed 1951 by Administrators C.T.A. of Kahlil Gibran Estate and Mary G. Gibran. Used by permission of Alfred A. Knopf, an imprint of the Knopf Doubleday Publishing Group, a division of Random House LLC. All rights reserved.

Library of Congress Cataloging-in-Publication Data

Goswami, Amit.
  Quantum creativity : think quantum, be creative / Amit Goswami. -- 1st edition.
    pages cm
  Includes bibliographical references and index.
  ISBN 978-1-4019-4075-1 (pbk.)
  1. Creative ability. 2. Creative thinking. 3. Creative ability in business. 4. Quantum theory. I. Title.
  BF408.G639 2014
  153.3'5--dc23
                              2013033280

Tradepaper ISBN: 978-1-4019-4075-1

17 16 15 14   5 4 3 2
1st edition, March 2014
2nd edition, March 2014

Printed in the United States of America

CONTENTS

PREFACE

Some of the results of my early exploration of a new understanding of reality based on quantum physics were published more than a decade ago in a book titled *Quantum Creativity*. It was written for scholars with the purpose of inviting academic researchers to consider quantum thinking in their exploration of creativity. This book draws on that earlier volume, hence the title, but this time I've written for the layperson interested in seeing creativity, which includes the way we shape our life experience, in an entirely new way. By becoming aware of our role in a creative universe based on consciousness, we can align ourselves with the evolution of consciousness at a time when life on our planet is under duress.

My first adult experience of creativity occurred a year after I came from India to Case Western Reserve University in Cleveland, Ohio, as a young instructor and postdoctoral researcher in theoretical physics. I was working hard on research into a new kind of interactive phenomenon concerning atomic nuclei, but I wasn't making any progress. That day I had discussed the subject with my mentor, only to have him poke such serious holes in my research that it no longer held together even in my prejudiced eyes. Despondent, I retired to the Snakepit, the school's basement cafeteria, nearly ready to give up my research altogether. Then the solution suddenly came to me with such clarity that I knew it had to be right. I raced upstairs to my mentor, who immediately saw its value. I still remember the euphoric haze in which I spent the rest of the afternoon.

I continued my research in nuclear physics for ten more years after that incident, solved a great many problems, and wrote quite a few scientific papers, but rediscovering the joy of that day seemed to elude me. Gradually, I became a little cynical. I assumed, like most of my colleagues, that scientific research is creative, but that creativity is not necessarily joyful. People who reported such joy probably exaggerated; my own memorable experience was perhaps due to a beginner's naive exuberance. I began to believe that creative work brought only the mature satisfaction that I felt each time I succeeded in solving a seemingly intractable problem, or writing another paper to further my career.

Then a major life change was precipitated by a divorce and the loss of a research grant, followed by remarriage and my decision to leave nuclear physics. I wrote a textbook on basic physics and then a book that explored the physics of science fiction. At some point I changed my research field to the interpretation of quantum mechanics.

Quantum mechanics, the 20th century's new paradigm of physics that replaced Sir Isaac Newton's "classical" physics, is used mostly to calculate the movement of submicroscopic objects (such as atoms, nuclei, and elementary particles), but actually holds for all material objects. In physics, the word *quantum* means a discrete quantity; a quantum of energy is an indivisible bundle of energy, for example.

Quantum mechanics rose over the horizon in the 1920s, and ever since, this new physics has threatened the worldview of science that is based on the idea that everything real is made of matter (any phenomenon that looks nonmaterial is illusory). But when we tried to explain quantum phenomena while holding on to this strict materialism, we were thwarted by paradoxes. It was these paradoxes that I set my mind to resolve.

After years of trepidation and false starts, I realized one evening during a discussion with a friend that the only way to resolve the quantum paradox was to break away completely from the current materialist paradigm, already irreparably damaged by quantum mechanics. A new premise composed of the idea that consciousness—not matter—is the true foundation of being would give rise to a reinvigorated science capable of moving beyond its previous limitations into exciting new territory. I also noticed that this discovery filled me with the same intense joy that I had experienced in the Snakepit cafeteria.

As I fleshed out this new consciousness-based paradigm of science, I realized that developing a comparable approach to creativity, an approach that inspired everyone to transcend their self-imposed limitations, was going to be of paramount importance. Creativity—like love, joy, inner peace, and many other intangibles that make life worthwhile—is a phenomenon that had been looked upon with suspicion by materialists, according to whom everything that happens is causally related to the past and nothing truly new is possible. My personal experiences had already told me otherwise, so I welcomed the challenge to push the limits of materialism and to transcend them.

Soon a colleague, Nora Cohen, and I founded a creativity research group at the University of Oregon (where I work) and began having regular meetings. Shortly after, a behavioral psychologist, Shawn Boles, and an anthropologist, Richard Chaney, joined the group. Nora, Shawn, Richard, and I formed a bond that was strengthened when we agreed to jointly write a book on creativity. Although the book was never completed (our differences in approach were too great to find common ground), I learned a tremendous amount from this collaboration about the existing theories and data regarding the phenomenon of creativity.

Shawn and I did agree about an important aspect of handling and classifying the diverse data on creativity. We both thought that creative work must be classified in two basic categories: one that is closer to problem solving (akin to technological invention), and another that involves the discovery of deeper truth. Many of the differences in creativity research arise because only one of these two different classes of creativity is addressed. Somewhere along the line I also recognized that spiritual growth is "inner" creativity, as contrasted to creativity in the arts and the sciences, which is "outer" creativity.

Meanwhile, Nora organized two research conferences on the theories of creativity. There I met many exponents of creativity research and witnessed the deep division that exists among them. However, developing a synthesis of these disparate ideas had to wait until the new consciousness-based paradigm was developed further. When my contribution to that effort, a book called *The Self-Aware Universe,* went to the printer, I was finally free to work on the various ways we think of creativity and how we approach it, both personally and socially. This book is the result of that work.

When we recognize consciousness as the central theme of the universe, it becomes clear that creativity is our lifeline to that consciousness. Then we begin to see how each of the different types of creativity has a role to play in embracing our full potential. And yes, we see clearly that creativity is not restricted to geniuses; all of us have the potential to be creative, and at any age.

Traditionally, the West has favored outer creativity over inner, and the East has preferred inner to outer. Past societies may have underplayed invention as a way of achieving social change, but present societies, with their consumer orientation, emphasize invention far too much. Such polarization keeps us from achieving our full potential, not to mention that none of these individual ways of harvesting creativity will be sufficient to the tasks of the 21st century. So the theme of this book, in the final reckoning, is the creative song with all its different harmonies. When we sing this music of creativity, using whichever harmony is appropriate to a particular endeavor, then our individual voices become part of the all-inclusive cosmic multiverse.

Besides the people already mentioned who played important roles in my research, I am grateful to Paul Ray, Howard Gruber, Kathy Juline, Robert Tompkins, Shawn Boles, Jean Burns, and Ligia Dantes for thoughtful readings of the manuscript. Thanks are also due to Ann Sterling, Michael Fox, and Anna St. Clair for helpful comments. Maggie Free's help with the editing was crucial, and all but one of the poems at the end of the chapters are the products of our joint collaboration. The help of Don Ambrose, Joe Giove, and Nan Robertson with the figures is gratefully acknowledged.

I'd also like to thank Ri Stuart for some helpful discussions that led to a revision of some of my own orthodoxy. I give special thanks to Renee Slade for a thorough preliminary editing and many helpful suggestions for improving the manuscript. I thank my wife Uma for her ongoing contributions to my own struggles with inner creativity. My special thanks to Peter Guzzardi for his wise editing. I thank Patty Gift at Hay House for her commitment to my work and her sage publishing counsel, and of course the production staff at Hay House, without whose careful cooperation this new book would not see the light of day.

PART I

STEPS TO UNDERSTANDING HUMAN CREATIVITY

CHAPTER 1

Is There a Science of Human Creativity?

Imagine yourself walking along an empty beach on a clear spring day, deep in thought. You've been grappling with life's big questions. From some distance away a man in a colorful hat approaches, and as he draws close you see a distinguished demeanor that gives him an air of wisdom, and the twinkle in his eye makes him seem approachable.

To your embarrassment you blurt out the question you've been posing to yourself. "I've been reading about how quantum physics has changed everything we've ever known about the way things work. But how can knowing about subatomic particles affect my choices about how I live my life?"

Astonishingly, the stranger doesn't seem to think you're crazy. In fact, he stops to consider your question, and then takes a seat on a nearby sand dune. After a few thoughtful moments, he responds. "Quantum physics is the physics of possibilities," he says gravely. "And not just material possibilities, but also possibilities of meaning, of feeling, and of intuiting. You choose everything you experience from these possibilities, so quantum physics is a way of understanding your life as one long series of choices that are in themselves the ultimate acts of creativity."

For some reason it doesn't seem odd that you should be engaging this total stranger in a profound metaphysical conversation. "But that sounds like just another way of saying 'We create our own reality.'

Don't get me wrong. I'm as fond of feel-good slogans as the next guy, but I just haven't found a way to make this one work for me."

"You're right; it's not that simple. But here's the thing. Quantum physics explains how our creative process involves both the conscious realm of manifest reality—what we see when we look around—and the realm of possibility, or pure potentiality. And unconscious possibilities also give rise to creative expression. This is the reason some creative experiences are called 'aha moments.' But we're not talking about a linear process. The reason why people assign such mystery to the ability to create something new can be seen in the context of a quantum leap—the kind of discontinuity we see when electrons leap from one atomic orbit to the next. But what I find most intriguing is the promise that once we understand the creative process as an expression of quantum physics we will have found a portal for accessing extraordinary creativity in every aspect of life. Anyone should be able to manifest whatever they choose; at least that's how I see it."

You start to feel hopeful. "I'd like to believe you, but I don't know much about physics. Are these ideas supported by scientific research?"

"Yes. The theory of quantum creativity is backed up by ample empirical evidence, and so is the impact it has on your life. Do you have any more questions? Make them succinct, and I promise to give you succinct answers. And if you're interested, I'll give you a copy of my book, as long as you promise to read it."

"Okay. First question. I know creativity is about coming up with something new, but that seems awfully basic. How would you define it?"

"Well, I'd say that creativity involves three things: discovering or inventing new meaning that has value—new or old, in new or old context(s)—or combinations thereof. Think of Mona Lisa's smile."

"Okay, but when you talk about meaning, are you just talking about science, mathematics, philosophy, the fine arts, and such? Just learning the basics in any one of these fields would take years, not to mention becoming an expert. Why would anyone invest so much time and effort with no guarantee that they'll succeed in contributing new meaning?"

"That's a good question. When our civilization was young, the exploration of meaning almost always produced something new. Almost everybody's life was creative then; like children, we were always discovering or inventing. As civilizations grow older, our knowledge systems become more sophisticated, yet it's still true that whenever we go into uncharted contextual territory, simplicity returns. As you'll see when you read my book, the new quantum worldview is based on the primacy of consciousness rather than matter; this is such a dramatic shift in perspective that even the sophisticated fields you mentioned are now wide open for creative exploration."

"I've read a little about that idea that we're all living in a sea of consciousness," you break in.

"I'm glad, because we're going to need everyone to participate in this new way of seeing things; it's our only chance to cope with the global crisis we're facing. Crisis has always been a clarion call to wake up to our creative potential. Are you ready to help?"

"Yes, I am."

"Einstein once said something to the effect that we cannot solve our problems from the same state of understanding from which they were created. So we need a change in worldview. And we're finding it in quantum physics."

"I see what you're saying. When the paradigm shifts, we go back to basics, which means that it's easier for ordinary people like me to contribute."

"Exactly. I will tell you a story. A pundit hires a boatman to take him across a broad river. An expert in Hindi, the pundit can't resist demonstrating his superiority. 'Have you learned much grammar, my dear man?' he asks the boatman. 'No, sir,' answers the boatman.

"'In that case half your life has been lost,' declares the pundit grandiosely. The boatman rows on, then suddenly the pundit notices his shoes are wet. Then the boatman asks, 'Have you learned any swimming, sir?' 'No,' says the pundit. 'In that case all of your life is lost,' the boatman replies. 'We're sinking.'

"What I'm trying to say with this story is that we're all equals in the new science, and in fact archetypal values themselves are open to creative exploration. What we historically call spiritual exploration is just another form of creativity, in this case inner creativity. It doesn't demand sophisticated knowledge systems, although some may be helpful, but it does require a commitment to developing our emotional intelligence, which has long been undervalued.

"When we apply quantum physics to ourselves, one of the surprises we discover is that our behaviors are no longer limited to the effects of genetics or the environment because our learned propensities are stored not only as brain memory; they are also stored outside of space and time, nonlocally, in such a way that we can continue to use them as we reincarnate again and again. The truth is that you and I have lived many lifetimes in order to develop the rational and emotional intelligence we have today."

"I've always been fascinated by reincarnation," you say.

"And rightly so. There is both theory and data supporting it."

"You're making me more and more curious about your book."

"Then I won't spend any more time building my case," the man says with a smile. "Let me leave you with one last thought. Evolution is fundamentally creative, and when we align ourselves with the evolutionary movements of consciousness, the universe itself puts wind in our sails. Quantum thinking goes beyond the thoughts we're aware of; it includes unconscious processing, which doesn't just expand our boundaries, but can also free us from the suffering that conscious processing (sometimes known as 'the monkey mind') creates."

"I presume your book will explain all this in more detail. I'm looking forward to reading it," you say, and hopefully you mean it.

How you see the world depends
On your worldview—your conceptual lens.
Be aware, my friend.
If your lens is not ground true,
Your world may look mechanical or dualistic.
With such worldviews
Creativity withers untended.
Polish your lens with quantum consciousness
And gaze once more through the eyes of the creative.

CHAPTER 2

Human Creativity and Differing Worldviews

Scientific materialism has shaped modern science and Western society for the better part of the last one hundred years. By emphasizing the external world, materialism has excluded the relevance of our internal experiences of feeling, meaning, and intuition. Which in turn has marginalized the arts, the humanities, ethics, religion, and spirituality—indeed, our consciousness itself—both in the academy and in society at large. God has been declared a delusion, and in a wave of cynicism people have lost not just their religious faith but also their belief in intangible values—love, goodness, justice, beauty, and even truth.

Modern science originated from the struggle to break free of the religious dogma of medieval Christianity: a wrathful God ruling over heaven doling out rewards and punishments when we die. Unfortunately, the materialist philosophy of science is also dogma. Make no mistake about it; there is no scientific evidence to support the claim that everything is matter. In fact, there is much evidence to the contrary.

So one dogma has given way to another: that consciousness is operational, mere language; that the psychology of the unconscious is touchy-feely voodoo; that mind is only brain; that there is nothing to feelings and intuitions other than what value arises from their role in Darwinian evolution; that there is nothing to the self other than psychosocial and genetic conditioning.

If the self does not exist, if consciousness is a mirage, if there is no other source of causation than material interaction, how can we take the ultimate creative step? How can we make profound changes in ourselves? To understand human creativity we need a new paradigm that includes both matter *and* consciousness; it must be inclusive of all human modes of experience—sensing, feeling, thinking, and intuition. We have discovered such an inclusive paradigm. We call it science within consciousness. It is based on quantum physics and the metaphysics that posits consciousness as the foundation of all being.

As a young adult, the psychologist William James was depressed by his belief that the deterministic philosophy of reality—that every movement is determined by physical laws—was correct. He was actually ill for several years. Then he discovered the philosophy of free will, and decided that his first act of free will should be to believe in free will. That decision brought him not just good health, but also a lifetime of creativity.

Today we're seeing an epidemic of depression because people can't find fulfillment in the spiritual and emotional void of the materialist worldview. Fortunately, the antidote is on its way. It is now clear that accepting the implications of quantum physics means making a basic change in our scientific worldview, from the primacy of matter to the primacy of consciousness. Here are some fundamental aspects of this new science.[1]

- Consciousness is the foundation of all being.

- Manifest matter is preceded by quantum possibilities or potentialities. There are two realms of reality— potentiality and actuality. Conscious choice collapses the possibilities into manifest actuality. Since this choice is made from a state of consciousness beyond the ego, we refer to it as a "higher" or "quantum" consciousness, spiritual traditions refer to it as God. And since our conscious choices are shaped by higher consciousness this process can be described by the term *downward causation.*

- Within one undivided consciousness, there are four worlds of quantum possibilities: the material world that we navigate with our senses, the vital world whose energies we feel, the mental world in which we think and process meaning, and the world of supramental archetypes that we intuit—truth, beauty, love, etc.

- Conscious choice precipitates the collapse of quantum possibilities (waves) of each world into the manifest realm (of actualities). The multiple parallel worlds do not directly interact; consciousness mediates their interaction (figure 1).

- The collapse is nonlocal, meaning that it requires no local communication or exchange of signals. The need for local communication via signals holds true only for space-time; quantum consciousness is nonlocal and therefore outside of space and time.

- The quantum collapse from possibility to actuality is discontinuous. The word *transcendent*, which we apply to the realm of pure potentiality, evokes both nonlocality and discontinuity.

- In the transcendent quantum realm of pure potentiality, consciousness remains undivided from its possibilities and there is no experience. Collapse produces "dependent co-arising" of an experiencing subject and an object that is experienced.

- Creativity is fundamentally a phenomenon of consciousness discontinuously manifesting *truly* new possibilities from transcendent potentiality. This is why in ancient traditions, creativity is referred to as a marriage between (transcendent) heaven and (immanent) earth.

- The mind gives meaning to the interaction of consciousness and matter.

- The value of creative work comes from what we intuit, what Plato called archetypes.

- The role of the brain is to make representations of mental meaning.

- Creativity is invention or discovery of new meaning. What is truly new is meaning invented or discovered using old or new archetypal contexts and combinations thereof.

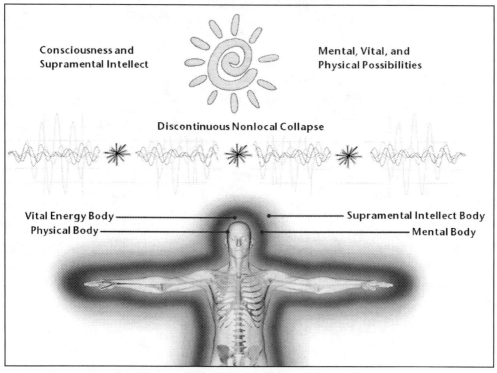

Figure 1: How psychophysical parallelism and
downward causation create all four of our experiences

When we use the new paradigm of science within consciousness to understand creativity, we make room for everyone willing to accept their own central role in creating the experience of their lives. It also tells us about the role conditioning plays, and what you can do about that. Creativity involves the causal power of consciousness choosing from quantum possibilities. If you learn to access this causal power and learn to manifest its message, you can create any and every aspect of the life experience you desire.

Freud and Jung were right when they said that creativity has much to do with our unconscious, which they defined as the repository of repressed stuff—personal and collective respectively. Quantum physics has given us an even broader picture of the unconscious: as the unmanifest—the realm of possibilities.

For most of us, creative motivation requires a crisis—either externally, like a threat to our physical survival, or an internal crisis of intense suffering. But how does curiosity become so strong for some people even in the absence of crisis? One answer may be a particularly close connection to one or more of the values that most inspire us: love, beauty, justice, goodness, and truth. As you travel on your own creative journey, your curiosity to know an archetype will gain traction. And as it does, evolution itself will be served. In the new science, evolution has a purposeful aspect that Darwin suspected but could not include in his theory—to express and manifest the archetypes in human experience and living. Or, to put it more poetically, to manifest heaven on earth. As we attune ourselves to the evolutionary purpose of the universe, our curiosity becomes ever more intense.

Here, in brief, is the central theme of this book. We create our own lives through the creative choices we make, which collapse new potentiality into actuality. This process can be understood, and we can become more skillful at it. The new theory of evolution tells us that by embracing the creative journey of this lifetime we are furthering the purpose of the evolutionary movement of consciousness. Knowing this makes our motivation all the keener.

What Is Quantum Creativity Good For?

So what can quantum creativity do for you and me that mechanical cut-and-paste creativity cannot deliver?

- Quantum creativity enables us to solve unusual problems that require holistic solutions, such as the degradation of the environment.

- Quantum creativity enables us to explore the meaning of our life and the meaning of the world around us. It awakens us to the creative evolution of consciousness on our planet.

- Quantum creativity allows us to not only explore archetypes but also to embody them.

- Quantum creativity enables us to explore firsthand the three great quantum principles: the already-mentioned discontinuity and nonlocality, and a third one, tangled hierarchy (see chapter 3). The exploration of discontinuity teaches us intelligence in general; the exploration of nonlocality teaches us ecological intelligence; the exploration of tangled hierarchy teaches us emotional intelligence.

- Quantum creativity compels us to learn how to function in the presence of real freedom, which teaches us real responsibility.

- Quantum creativity enables us to integrate our outer and inner life.

- Quantum creativity enables us to achieve spiritual fulfillment.

- And quantum creativity can help make you rich and famous, if that's what you're looking for.

The genie of true creativity is bottled up in most of us—to liberate it is to become the architect of our own lives. Understanding what human creativity entails, what role it plays in our self-development, how our creative processes work, and where our motivation comes from, will assist many of us to scale the barriers to our imprisoned self in order to experience joy and make a difference in the world. Can your creativity express itself as potently as Einstein's or Gandhi's? It's up to you.

Thinking about creativity?
Asking questions?
Your questions are firefly glimpses
Of the soul calling you.

Do you hear the lapping of possibility waves
On the shore of your mind?
Then look through the quantum window.
Face-to-face with your original self
The quantum leap will take you by surprise.

CHAPTER 3

This Is the Mount the Creative Rides: The Quantum

In a famous anecdote, impressionist artist René Magritte once went into a store and wanted to buy some Dutch cheese. As the storekeeper reached over to get some from the display window, Magritte insisted that he would rather have a piece cut from a wheel in an inside case. "But they are the same cheese," exclaimed the storekeeper. "No, madam," said Magritte. "The one in the window has been looked at all day by crowds of people passing by."

You might dismiss Magritte as a kooky artist, but in the new thinking inspired by quantum physics, objects are just possibilities for consciousness to choose from, a choice made when we measure them by simply looking. This seems to support Magritte; looking changes things. In fact, it changes *everything.*

But how? It is, to say the least, puzzling. And that's a good thing. Quantum physics should have that effect on us. As physicist Niels Bohr once said, if you're not puzzled by quantum physics, you couldn't possibly have understood it.

Let's begin from the beginning. What does it mean when we say a quantum object exists as potentiality or possibility? Consider an electron. Measuring its location requires an experimental apparatus like a

Geiger counter. The researcher sets up a three-dimensional grid of Geiger counters in the room where we've released our electron. In a given measurement only one of the Geiger counters will tick—the electron will show up at one place. In another measurement the electron will trigger a Geiger counter at a different location. If we make a very large number of these measurements, the electron's positions will look like a bell curve (figure 2), which turns out to agree with quantum physics' predictions. So in its potential form the electron is everywhere in the room, but during a given observation it manifests at only one place.

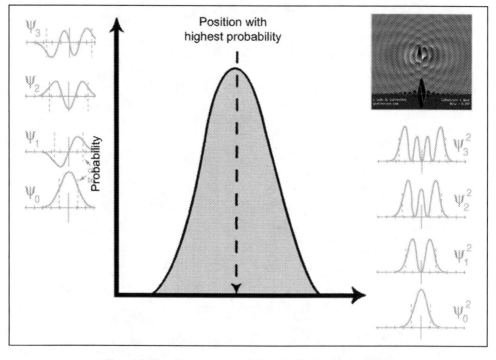

Figure 2: The electron's probability distribution (bell curve)

Okay, you may be thinking, that's odd, but not unfathomable. Wait. There's more. A Geiger counter is itself made up of subatomic particles, all of which are also possibility waves. *So the tool we're using to locate our electron is also just a possibility.* Possibility coupled to possibility only gives you greater possibility. Even you, the human observer, the experimenter, are made up of possible elementary particles.

When coupled with the electron and the Geiger counter, your presence generates an even bigger wave of possibility, but no actuality (figure 3).

Why is it that in the presence of a human observer, one Geiger counter or another in the grid always ticks? What is the explanation of this *observer effect?*

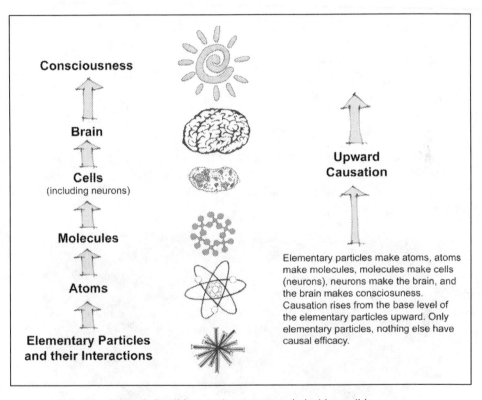

Consciousness

Brain

Cells
(including neurons)

Molecules

Atoms

Elementary Particles and their Interactions

Upward Causation

Elementary particles make atoms, atoms make molecules, molecules make cells (neurons), neurons make the brain, and the brain makes consciosuness. Causation rises from the base level of the elementary particles upward. Only elementary particles, nothing else have causal efficacy.

Figure 3: Possible consciousness, coupled with possible objects, produces even bigger possibilities, not actuality.

Puzzling? No doubt about it. This quantum measurement paradox has given quantum physicists sleepless nights for decades. The paradox thickens when you learn that a theorem attributed to the mathematician John von Neumann states that no material interaction can ever convert possibility into actuality. Von Neumann argued that a human observer is made up of more than just elementary particles; an observer also possesses consciousness—the facility for knowing.

This consciousness chooses one facet out of a many-faceted wave of possibility and collapses it to one particular facet; for the electron above, this means one particular position.

Paradox solved? Yes, but now we've replaced it with another. How does consciousness interact with the material electron to do its choosing? Any interaction should require a signal carrying energy, but consciousness doesn't appear to have this quality. The answer is this: consciousness is the foundation of all being, including matter; when choosing from material possibilities, consciousness is choosing from itself and therefore doesn't require a signal.

For an analogy, look at my favorite picture in figure 4 of two meanings—a young woman and an old woman—among the same lines that the artist named "My wife and my mother-in-law." When we see one image—the young woman or the old—and then shift our perspective of looking to see the other image, we are not doing something to the picture. The possibility of seeing both meanings is already there in our mind. We are just recognizing and choosing one of our own possibilities.

Figure 4: A gestalt picture, *My wife and my mother-in-law,* originally by W. E. Hill.

This theory can be verified if we can empirically show that signal-free, or nonlocal, communications indeed exist. As it happens, since 1935 quantum physicists have been aware of this "weird" possibility that quantum physics allows nonlocal communications. In quantum physics we can correlate two different objects by letting them inter-act for a bit in close proximity. Quantum math shows that afterward the objects remain interconnected, or capable of nonlocal signal-less communication—even when they are not interacting and are sepa-rated by vast distances (figure 5). Nonlocal correlations exist in a do-main of interconnectedness that transcends space and time.

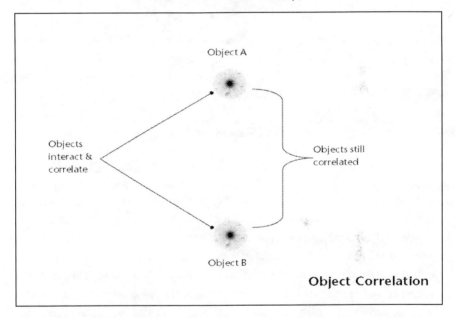

Figure 5: If two quantum objects interact, they become correlated in such way as to communicate even at a distance when they are not interacting.

Even if we accept this quantum weirdness in the world of atomic particles, it seems preposterous to expect nonlocality in the larger ev-eryday world in which we live. If correlation between people worked the same way as correlation between photons, then when two people interact in some way and then move to opposite ends of the earth, if one of them touches a cactus and feels the prick, the other one should feel the prick as well (figure 6).

Figure 6: Does the miracle of nonlocal correlations apply to people?
If two people are correlated at some origin, if one of them hits a cactus,
will the other feel a prick, too? Or is this just a metaphor?

There's evidence that this absurd idea is not far from the truth. Experiments by the Mexican neurophysiologist Jacobo Grinberg-Zylberbaum and his collaborators, along with some two dozen other experiments, directly support the idea of quantum nonlocal connection between human brains.[1] Typically in these experiments, two subjects are instructed to meditate together for a period of 20 minutes in order to establish "direct communication," or correlation; then they enter separate Faraday chambers (enclosures that block all electromagnetic signals) for the duration of the experiment, all the while meditating on direct communication.

Their brains are then connected to individual electroencephalogram (EEG) machines. One of the subjects is now shown a series of light flashes that produce electrical activity in his or her brain. From the recordings of an EEG attached to this brain, experimenters extract a signal called an evoked potential. Amazingly, in approximately one in four cases the unstimulated partner's brain also shows electrical activity similar in shape and strength to the evoked potential. Control subjects who do not meditate together or are not able to establish and maintain direct communication never show any transferred potential (figure 7).

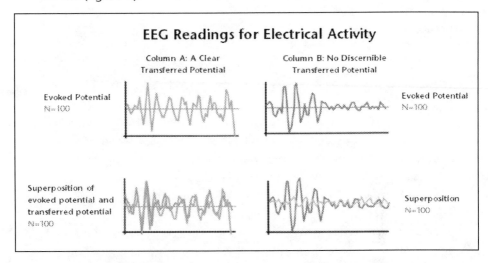

Figure 7: Transferred potential. Column A: In Grinberg-Zylberbaum's experiment, if two subjects are correlated and one of them is shown a series of light flashes that produces a distinct evoked potential measured by the EEG attached to his scalp, a transferred potential of comparable strength and phase appears in the nonstimulated partner's EEG as well. Column B: A control subject without correlation, even when there is a distinct evoked potential in the stimulated subject's EEG, shows no transferred potential.

The straightforward explanation is that the two brains act as a nonlocally "correlated" or "entangled" quantum system. In response to a stimulus to only one of the correlated brains, nonlocal quantum consciousness collapses close-to-identical states in the two brains. Clearly, there is a striking similarity between correlated photons and correlated brains, but there is also a striking difference. In the former case, as soon as the possibility wave is collapsed by measurement, the objects become uncorrelated; however, in the case of the correlated brains, consciousness maintains the correlation over the 100 or so light flashes needed to get the average evoked potential.

This difference is highly significant. The nonlocality of correlated photons, although striking in terms of demonstrating the radicalness of quantum physics, cannot be used to transfer information. But in the case of correlated brains, based on the transferred brain potential, an experimenter could easily conclude that the correlated partner of the transferee has seen the optical stimulus; this is information.

If You Are Looking for the Secret of Manifestation

The popular book and movie *The Secret* tells people that in order to manifest what they want in life, all they need to do is form the right intention. Based on this principle, things we want will be attracted to us; we don't need to do anything but sharpen our intention. Well, before *The Secret* came along, there were New Agers in the '70s who tried to manifest whatever they wanted (an ounce of pot, perhaps?) when they heard the von Neumann message of quantum physics, distilled by physicist Fred Alan Wolf: We create our own reality. But of course the free pot never materialized.

What went wrong? We have a long way to go before we refine this ability into something practical, but one obstacle is that we try to do it all at the ego level of the mind, and for personal advantage. According to a growing school of thought, your intention has a much better chance of being supported by nonlocal quantum consciousness if it serves the greater good.

Multiple Creativity

If we apply the idea of nonlocality to the creative act, it follows that two people may have the same creative idea across space and time without any local contact between them. Evidence for this kind of correlated creativity is found in the many instances of major discoveries having been made simultaneously by two or more people separated in space and time.

Werner Heisenberg, a young man in his twenties, discovered that if he took the possible quantum jumps in an atom and arranged them in an array, these quantities obeyed an equation that no classical physicist had ever seen, but that had all the new properties expected for the new physics. These arrays were known in mathematics; they are called matrices. But Heisenberg had never heard of them and seldom had anybody used such quantities in physics. They are very different from ordinary numbers. If you multiply 3 by 4, you get 12; if you multiply 4 by 3, you still get 12. For ordinary numbers, the order of multiplication makes no difference—a property called commutativity. Heisenberg's new quantum quantities, the matrices, do not commute; for them the order in which you perform their multiplication does make a difference. It's a little like the dating scene where the order in which you ask the two questions "Do you like me?" and "Do you love me?" matters very much.

After attending a seminar on the wave-nature of matter that physicist Louis de Broglie discovered, chemist Peter Debye commented to physicist Erwin Schrödinger that if matter is a wave, there must be a mathematical "wave equation" that applies to matter. Debye himself forgot about his quip; but his comment inspired Schrödinger to the discovery of the equation for matter waves (now called the Schrödinger equation). It was the same discovery as Heisenberg's, but in a different form, as demonstrated by another great quantum physicist, Paul Dirac. Similarly, the nearly simultaneous discovery of calculus by Isaac Newton and Gottfried Leibniz is another example of multiple creativity if we are not fooled by the difference of form. Nonlocality refers to both space and time; the events of multiple discovery do not have to be simultaneous.

There are also anecdotal reports of nonlocality of a different kind. Novelist Isabel Allende had an amazing experience while writing her second novel, *Of Love and Shadows,* about a political crime in Chile in 1973. The military had killed 15 people and hidden their bodies in an abandoned mine, where they were discovered years later by the Catholic Church. Unable to learn details about how the discovery happened, Allende filled them in from her imagination; a priest heard the details of the killing in a confession, went to the mine, and took pictures, wrapping them up in his blue sweater to keep them hidden. Years later a Jesuit priest came to her and corroborated her imagined story even to the last detail—wrapping the photos in his blue sweater. "I think there is a prophetic or clairvoyant quality in writing," Allende says.

In the same vein, while novelist Alice Walker was writing *The Temple of My Familiar,* she felt "connected with the ancient knowledge that we all have, and that it was really a matter not of trying to learn something, but of remembering." It's another nice example of quantum nonlocality over time.

Discontinuity: Taking the Quantum Leap

Although there is much data suggesting that discontinuity is a feature of creative insights, some researchers have difficulty accepting this. If you are having similar difficulty, consider the work of Niels Bohr. When an electron jumps orbits in an atom, said Bohr, it does not travel through the intervening space (figure 8); first the electron is here, and then it's there. It disappears from the old orbit and reappears in the new without passing through the space in between. Instantaneously. Much the way a pumpkin becomes a carriage right before Cinderella's disbelieving eyes, or Merlin casts the magic sword Excalibur into a block of stone.

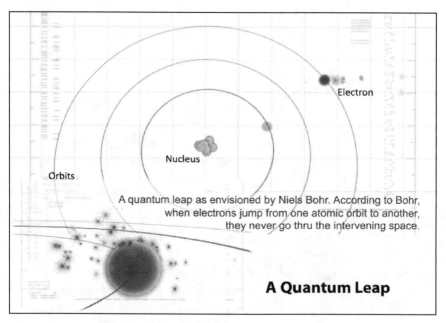

Figure 8. The quantum leap. Light is emitted only when the electron discontinuously jumps (denoted by "pop") from an upper to a lower orbit. The atomic orbits can be thought of as the rungs of a quantum ladder. The electron pops out of an upper orbit and pops into a lower one discontinuously.

Can we understand quantum physics without this magic, without these quantum jumps? At first Schrödinger, who co-discovered quantum physics, refused to accept discontinuity. When he visited Niels Bohr in Copenhagen, Schrödinger protested for days against quantum jumps. Eventually, however, he conceded the point with this emotional outburst: "If I had known that one has to accept this damned quantum jump, I'd never have gotten involved with quantum physics." To this Bohr replied, "But we are all glad that you did."

Where Your Creative Intentions Work

So why do we find the cosmos out there and the cabbages down here almost exactly where we expect them according to Newtonian physics? Am I asking you to believe that the room you are in, the desk you work at, this earth under the sun, all disappear from existence when nobody is looking? Not quite. Quantum physicists aren't saying that everything winks out of existence when we look away. It still exists, but only as potentiality.

In addition, the molecules of large massive objects are held together by cohesive forces, so they conduct their wave movements standing in place, much like a guitar string. In fact, quantum mathematics works in such a way that for massive objects as a whole the possibility spectrum is quite limited. A desk has very little leeway (calculations show that the center of mass of the desk may move in possibility in a sphere of roughly 10^{-16} cm or so), so whenever you look, you find the desk at basically the same place. And that's a good thing. A crucial aspect of the macro fixity (stability) of matter is that it supports the correlated existence of vital energies and mental meanings (through the lungs and vocal chords that give voice to speech, for instance). Finally, the fixity in the macro world gives us the objects we see as reference points!

Consciousness uses gross matter and subtle energy to perform its play. Ordinarily for matter, this play has a lot of fixity. However, when subtle energies engage with consciousness, then creativity is possible, even likely. In their quantum aspects both the brain and the mind consist of possibilities from which consciousness can create the endlessly new. Only when the quantum aspects of the brain and the mind are suppressed does conditioned behavior prevail.

Who Creates?

If consciousness is the foundation of being, if it is omnipresent, shouldn't potentiality be collapsing around us all the time? The presence of consciousness in itself does not cause potentiality to actualize. Collapse occurs when an observer with a brain is present as well, with the intention to look. Nonlocal consciousness that chooses always remains in potentiality, but the effect of the choice occurs in the manifest domain of actuality.

There is that old quantum measurement paradox. Collapse of the object into manifestation requires the presence of the observer (the subject of the experience of looking), but without collapse the observer (the subject) is also potentiality. This raises a "chicken or the egg"-type question: What comes first, the subject of awareness (that is having the experience) or the objects of awareness (which are being experienced)? The answer is neither; the subject and the object of the awareness are co-created by downward causation (choice) through the operation of quantum measurement in the brain. The crucial point here is to realize that the brain is very special. In the presence of the observer's brain, possibilities collapse, although we never see the brain at work; instead, we identify with it. This is because the brain has a "tangled hierarchy" built into it.

What is a tangled hierarchy? In a simple hierarchy a "lower" level affects a "higher" level; for example, a space heater heats the room, not the other way around. In the presence of simple feedback the upper level reacts in response (for example, if the space heater has a thermostat), but we still can tell what is higher and lower in the hierarchy. By contrast, in tangled hierarchies the levels of causality are so intertwined that we no longer can identify which is the lower level and which is the upper.

As an example of tangled hierarchy consider the following statement: *This sentence is false.* If the sentence is false, then it is actually true, which would mean it is false, and so on ad infinitum. But this infinite oscillation—a causal circularity—has made the sentence very special. We call such sentences self-referential. When you enter one you get caught in it; you identify with it.[2]

In the brain, perception requires memory, and memory requires perception. And we cannot establish how this causal circularity can come about through a system of higher and lower levels, as we did with the heater and the room. In other words, the work of the brain is a tangled hierarchy.

What happens when consciousness collapses the macroscopically distinguishable quantum possibility states of this tangled-hierarchical system of the brain? Self-identity. Consciousness identifies with the observer's brain, which thusly develops the capacity to refer to itself as separate from its environment.

This solution of the quantum measurement paradox also solves the paradox of perception, how *you* come into the theater of perception at all. When your brain identifies something outside yourself, it makes an image, no doubt, but who is looking at this image? A mini-you, a homunculus, sitting at the back of the brain? If so, then who is looking at the homunculus? The puzzle is solved by a tangled hierarchy: for the brain the observer becomes the observed; consciousness identifies with the brain, leaving the impression that there is just you looking at an object separate from you.

But notice that the loop created by the statement *This sentence is false* depends on certain implicit rules. The circularity of the sentence is not apparent to a child who asks, *Why* is this sentence false? The rules of English grammar and our adherence to them maintain the tangle; transcending the sentence means acting at an inviolate level, inviolate because it is not accessible to the sentence.

Similarly, in the observer effect the choosing quantum consciousness is implicit, not explicit. The observer-I, the apparent agent of the collapse, arises co-dependently with the external object. Acting from the transcendent realm of potentiality, quantum consciousness collapses the possibility wave of the tangled-hierarchical system of the brain, but we in manifest awareness cannot be aware of causing the collapse. This is like the famous Escher picture of drawing hands (figure 9): The left hand and the right hand seem to draw each other, but behind the curtain of the inviolate level, Escher is drawing them both. Similarly, the experiencer and the experienced, subject and object, appear to be co-creating one another, although in the final reckoning nonlocal consciousness is the only cause.

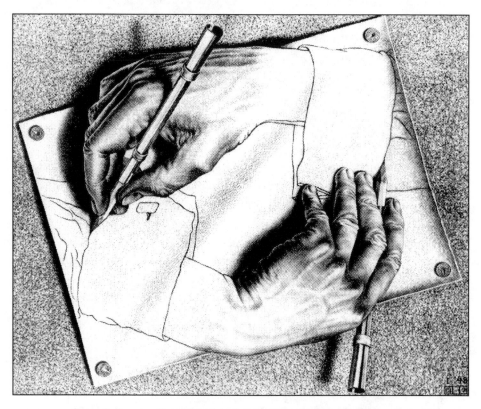

Figure 9: *Drawing Hands* by M. C. Escher. From the "immanent" reality of the paper, the left and the right hands appear to draw each other, but in truth from the transcendent inviolate level, Escher draws them both.

This self-creation is archetypally depicted as the *uroboros*—a snake biting its own tail: I choose, therefore I am. (See figure 10). This form of self-consciousness I call the quantum self, but it is known by many names in the spiritual traditions of the world. For example, Hindus refer to it by the Sanskrit word *atman,* and in Christianity it is called the Holy Spirit.

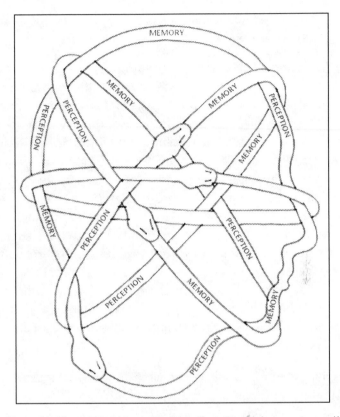

Figure 10: The tangled hierarchical manifestation of the quantum self

Who creates? You do, but in your quantum consciousness (that which our ancestors referred to as God), which is a state of unconscious being. This mode of being (the quantum consciousness) and this mode of experiencing (the quantum self) are important players in all acts of creation. Are they really two states of consciousness, two separate realms, separated by a discontinuity? There are many instances of creativity at the moment of waking up from sleep indicating that this is the case.

Consider the composer Richard Wagner's account of his discovery of the overture to *Das Rheingold.* Wagner came home after taking a walk and went to bed, but could not sleep for a while. His mind wandered through various musical themes and eventually he dozed.

Suddenly, he awoke and the overture of his famous *Rheingold* came to him in a creative outpouring.

> Returning [from a walk] in the afternoon, I stretched my-self, dead tired, on a hard couch, awaiting the long-desired hour of sleep. It did not come; but I fell into a kind of somno-lent state, in which I suddenly felt as though I was sinking in swiftly flowing water. The rushing sound formed itself in my brain into a musical sound, the chord of E-flat major, which continually re-echoed in broken forms; these broken forms seemed to be melodic passages of increasing motion, yet the pure triad of E-flat major never changed, but seemed by its continuance to impart infinite significance to the element in which I was sinking. I awoke in sudden terror from my doze, feeling as though the waves were rushing above my head. I at once recognized that the orchestral overture to the *Rheingold*, which must long have lain latent within me, though it had been unable to find definite form, had at last been revealed to me.[3]

So what is the role of the ego in all this? And what is the relation-ship of the quantum self with the ego?

Conditioning and the Ego

Experiences lead to learning, one aspect of which involves chang-es in the brain's substructure responsible for memories and represen-tations of experience. Something profound also takes place in the brain's quantum system. In response to a stimulus, the quantum ma-chinery of the brain not only interacts with the direct stimulus (the primary awareness event), but it also interacts repeatedly with the secondary stimuli of the memory replay; upon collapsing the possi-bilities this gives rise to secondary awareness events. These reflections in the mirror of memory act as feedback.

As a result of this feedback, the probability of actualizing certain formerly experienced states gradually gets higher and higher. The quantum brain gradually becomes conditioned in its response to previously learned stimuli. The probability distribution that previously was a bell curve becomes a sharp peak.

Where does our feedback-modified quantum brain's conditioned learning reside? The modification of the quantum dynamic is expressed as mathematical equations; these equations are not part of the brain, but they govern the behavior of a conditioned brain. Like any law of physics (of which the math is a mental representation), they reside in the nonlocal domain of consciousness that lies beyond the workings of the mind. *Quantum learning is based on local brain-memory, no doubt, but the propensity derived from the learning is nonlocal; it resides outside space and time.*

Fairly early in our physical development, learning accumulates and conditioned response patterns begin to dominate the brain's behavior, despite the fact that the versatility of the quantum system is always available for new creative play. If we don't engage the creative potency of the quantum system, if we don't attend to the primary-awareness events, the secondary-awareness processes, which are connected with memory-replay, begin to dominate. In this way the creative freedom of the tangled hierarchy of the brain is replaced by the conditioned simple hierarchy of learned programs. Then we begin to identify with a separate, individual self, the ego, which thinks it chooses on the basis of past experiences, presumably using "free will" for making its choices. But in truth, this so-called free will of the ego-identity exists only: 1) for choosing among the conditioned subset of possible responses; 2) to the extent that the conditioning for any particular response is less than 100 percent for saying "no" to conditioned choices. I call our ego "ice cream" consciousness; in answer to the question *What flavor of ice cream do you like?* you can: 1) choose chocolate, your first preference; and if that is not available go down the list—vanilla, strawberry, etc.—in order of your preferences; or 2) say "no" to your conditioned choices.

The Co-creator Roles of Quantum/Creative and Classical/ Determined Selves in Creativity

As we're seeing, an adult person is capable of operating in two modes of self-identity: the ego and the quantum self (figure 11). The classical ego mode, associated with our continuous, conditioned, and predictable behavior, augments our creative ideas and meanings with representations and learned contexts for expression. It enables us to develop and manipulate creative ideas and meanings into full-blown forms, and enjoys the fruits of our accomplishments. The quantum self is the experiencer of our intuitive insights into new meanings and new contexts, of the flashes of imagination that cannot be directly derived from prior learning.

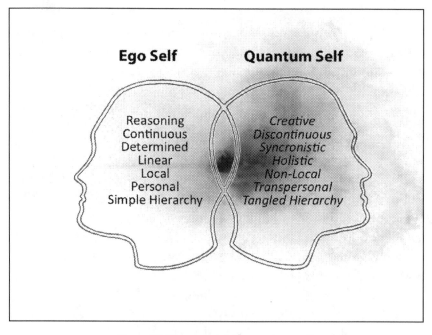

Figure 11: The ego and the quantum self

The ego and the quantum self are co-creators. There is a flow in the act of creation where writers, artists, athletes, musicians, even an occasional scientist, lose themselves, so thoroughly engaged are they with their acts. This blurring of the subject-object distinction could only indicate that in the creative flow the creator continually falls into the tangled hierarchy of the quantum self. The ego still operates in its manifesting capacity, but only in a secondary role.

Einstein said, there are two ways to live life. One is as if nothing is a miracle. The other is as if everything is a miracle. When we are completely stuck in the ego, nothing is a miracle. But when we take creative leaps with the quantum self, everything is a miracle.

The Quantum Nature of Thought

The mind processes thoughts, objects of meaning—but is the movement of thought quantum movement? Material quantum objects obey the uncertainty principle—we cannot simultaneously measure both their position and momentum with complete accuracy. In order to determine the trajectory of an object, we need to know not only where an object is now, but also where it will be a little later; in other words, both its position and momentum simultaneously. So we can also never determine accurate trajectories of material quantum objects.

Physicist David Bohm pointed out that an uncertainty principle operates also for thoughts. If we focus on the content of thought (as we do when we meditate on a mantra), we lose the direction the thought was taking; however, focusing on the direction of thought, as we do when we're free-associating, leads to a loss of content. Try it and see. The content of a thought is called its feature; the line of thought is its association.

So David Bohm's observation (and yours, if you have tried the little experiment) reveals that a thought is a quantum object that appears and moves in the field of our internal awareness just as physical objects appear and move in ordinary space. But thoughts appear in awareness only when we are actually thinking. Where does a thought go *between* measurements, between moments of thinking? It returns to its original state as a wave of possibilities of meaning. Exactly like material quantum objects, thoughts exist in consciousness as transcendent potentiality of many possible meanings; collapse manifests them in a form that now has complementary attributes, such as a specific feature and association.

The quantum picture forces us to think about the physical and mental worlds differently. Normally, we think of both these worlds as made up of substances. Yes, the mental substance is subtle—private; we cannot quantify it in the same way through consensus agreement as we can the physical, but it is still a substance, or so we think. We need to change this view. Even what we know to be physical is not a substance in the permanent sense, let alone what we know as mental. Both the physical and the mental worlds remain possibilities until consciousness gives them substance by collapsing them into an actual experience or object.

When I see a rose, there are two objects in my awareness. There is the external rose. This rose I can share with anyone else who may be looking at it; it is public. But along with that external rose there is a thought—the meaning I give to the experience of the external rose. This thought is internal and private. Only I am aware of it. My brain could be wired to EEG machines, opened up through surgery, or explored by magnetic resonance imaging for all to see. But no instrument could convey to anyone else the thoughts my internal awareness of the rose evoked. But how does this happen?

As consciousness recognizes and collapses a particular state from the quantum possibilities of the brain in response to a stimulus, it also recognizes and chooses the correlated mental meaning. Thus, in the process of perception, consciousness uses the brain to make representations not only of the physical world, but also of the mental meanings that come with it. The mental world is what physicists sometimes refer to as an infinite medium, made up of quantum possibility waves. In between collapses and experiences, mental modes are subject to rapid quantum movement: they quickly become large pools of possible meanings. This means that between my collapse and your collapse, between my thinking and your thinking, the quantum possibilities have expanded so much that it becomes extraordinarily unlikely that you will collapse the same thought that I will. In this way, thoughts are private; we experience them as internal.

Earlier in the chapter we discussed the conditioning of a brain response to a stimulus through the feedback mechanism of memory. Over time the correlated responses of the mind are also conditioned and individualized, allowing the mind to acquire a particular mental character as we go through life experiences of stimulus-response reinforcements. In other words, although you share the same potential mind with others (the quantum mind is an indivisible whole), your personal mind or ego forms as you acquire your own individual patterns of response.

A similar process gives us an individualized vital body in the vital world as the organs of our body become conditioned as an aspect of our growing up. These individualized vital and mental bodies allow you to bring individuality to your acts of creation.

In classical physics, conditioned certainty.
But in quantum physics, only ambiguous possibility,
There lies creativity.
Capable in your fixed classical modality,
You may rest on your laurels.
But yours is a unique condition:
Why fear ambiguity? It contains renewal.

Have you a strong ego?
Yes? Then take a risk, encounter your quantum self.
Go ahead—see what happens.
Newtonian chow is okay; but the taste is always the same.
For the truly delicious taste of creativity,
Savor quantum thinking.

CHAPTER 4

The Meaning of Mind

Look at the picture shown in figure 12. In image A, are you puzzling over what this might represent, other than a bunch of jagged lines? Could this be a broken picket fence with a couple of boards missing? What *do* those lines in the gap represent? Suppose we make up a story that fills in the details. Let's say a soldier is walking his dog behind the fence, but of course, at this moment, from this angle, we can see only his bayonet and his dog's tail! You see it, too, don't you?

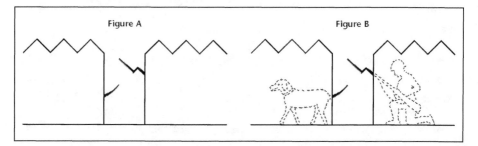

Figure 12: (a) What meaning do you see in the jagged lines?
(b) The artist's intended meaning.

This is a typical psychology-class exercise in how we make meaning. I've already argued that our brain's much-glorified neo-cortex cannot make meaning by itself; it is only a symbol-processing center. It is the *mind* that gives meaning to objects of the physical world, including the brain's symbols. To put this another way, a sentence has a structure, its syntax, which ensures that the words are put together in an orderly fashion. But the syntax will not enlighten you as to the meaning of the sentence, its semantic content. That's something extra.

Computers also jump from symbol processing to meaning/semantics. The meaning exists in the mind of the computer programmer, who then represents the meaning using the symbols in his or her software programs. Similarly, whenever our mind gives meaning to an object or stimulus—physical, vital, mental, or supramental—consciousness uses our brain to make a representation of the mental meaning. Whenever a brain representation is activated, our correlated mind plays out the associated meaning.

In our imaginations we make new meaning out of existing brain representations and their associated meanings in a continuous manner. How would you draw a picture, or sculpt a statue? You'd start with pencil and paper, to be sure, but you'd also need your imagination. You'd use it to come up with a mental picture of what you are going to draw or sculpt, using existing representations in the form of memory; only then does something happen between the brain, hand, pencil, and paper (or brain, fingers, and clay). This won't be original, of course; originality requires creativity—discontinuity, not continuity.

From a Brick to a Red Dress: The Context of Meaning

Could you make a red dress out of bricks? Adults often struggle to come up with an answer to this question. But a child might suggest that if we made a building with brick in its outer layer, the red brick could function as the building's red dress. This shift from the usual way of seeing brick exemplifies a change in context, and it's something that children, whose imaginations have not yet been limited by society, are particularly good at.

Etymologically, the word *context* comes from two Latin words—*com* (together), and *texere* (to weave). Context refers to the relationship of a system to its environment, of a figure to the ground on which the figure appears. Perhaps the most familiar experience you have with contexts is the way the meaning of a word changes when set against different verbal backgrounds. Consider the two sentences:

The ass is a useful domestic animal.
Anybody who does not appreciate context is an ass.

The word *ass* has a different meaning in the second sentence because it is used in a new context, in a new juxtaposition of words. Einstein gave a now-classic example of context in his argument that subjective time is not a fixed entity. If you sit on a hot stove for one minute, it will seem like an hour; but one hour with your sweetheart will seem like a minute.

Fundamental and Situational Creativity

Using this idea of contextual change, we now can distinguish between two kinds of creativity—fundamental and situational. Fundamental creativity yields a truly new and creative meaning because it is original in at least its archetypal context; additionally, there may be new physical and mental contexts as well. Now we have an unambiguous definition of fundamental creativity: the bringing into manifestation new meaning of archetypal value in a new context.

What is the new in situational creativity? Situational creativity is based on old archetypal contexts from which we have not extracted all meaning of value. Furthermore, when we combine old contexts, there is also the possibility of new meaning of value. So situational creativity consists of creating a new product or solving a problem in a way that reflects new meaning of value in an old archetypal context or a combination of old archetypal contexts. Additionally, new physical and mental contexts may be involved. The new meaning in situational creativity applies to the limited arena of a particular situation, whereas fundamental creativity encompasses many, many situations.

No computer algorithm can be given for recognizing new meaning, so situational creativity is also a property of the creative mind, although the meaning derived is not as revolutionary as in the shift to a new context. It is in their search for meaning of value that situational creatives succeed in finding novel solutions to problems. It is the novelty that separates situational creativity from problem solving.

There is some data that strongly suggest that mechanical problem solving is indeed not creativity, not even situational creativity. There are tests of creativity that measure a person's ability to think about a subject in as many contexts as possible; they ask such questions as, how many ways can you use a fan? How many titles can you come up with for a given story? If context hunting is what we do in creativity, then certainly this kind of "divergent thinking" test is provocative. And the tests are consistent: when a person takes this test again, he or she tends to get a similar score. But there seems to be no correlation between the test scores and the actual creativity of the person tested. The transition from trivial contexts of problem solving to meaningful contexts of creativity is anything but trivial.

To summarize, the essence of creativity, both fundamental and situational, involves consciousness, meaning, and value. Mechanistic theories of creativity cannot make room for any of these aspects. By invoking quantum physics within the framework that consciousness, not matter, is the foundation of all being, all these essential aspects of creativity are incorporated and yet the model is scientific.

Thinking Out of the Box: The Nine-Points Problem

Consider the following, called the nine-points problem:

What is the smallest possible number of straight lines that will connect the nine points of a 3 X 3 rectangular array (figure 13A) without taking the pencil off the paper? It seems that you need five lines (figure 13B), doesn't it? That's too many. Can you see how to get a smaller number of straight lines to do the job?

Probably not. Like most people, you likely think that you have to connect the points while staying within the boundary defined by the outer points of the rectangular array. If so, you have limited yourself to an unnecessary context for solving the problem; you are thinking in a box (literally), and you have to move out of the box to find a new, broader context in which a smaller number of straight lines will do the job (figure 13C). This idea of extending the boundary beyond the existing context—thinking out of the box—is crucially important in creativity. And sometimes creativity is as simple as recognizing that what is not forbidden may be allowed.

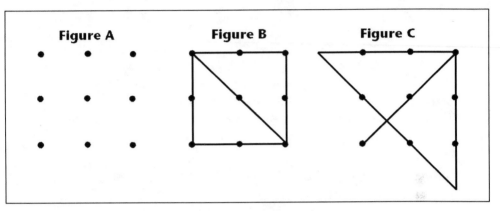

Figure 13: (a) The nine points problem. Connect the points with as few lines as you can without raising your pencil. (b) The solution that first occurs to many people. They think within the box of their existing belief system. (c) A better solution of the nine point problem. Extend your context. Think out of the box.

An Example of Fundamental Creativity: The Bohr Atom

In the early part of the 20th century physicist Ernest Rutherford combined the old context of the solar system with the new context of the atom. He saw that just as planets revolve around the sun as a result of the sun's gravitational attraction, electrons might revolve around the nucleus. This is a good example of situational creativity, but there is no fundamental creativity—at least not yet. The model has a problem. According to the laws of classical physics, the electrons, which lose energy by continuously emitting radiation, must eventually spiral down and crash into the nucleus. Rutherford's atom cannot be stable.

Niels Bohr found an unconventional answer to this dilemma outside the established context of the old Newtonian physics, thereby paving the way for a new physics. For Bohr, the orbits of the electrons in an atom are discrete and stationary; they are "quantized," frozen stations in space. The electrons emit radiation only when changing orbits, not while they're in these orbits (violating the rules of then-known physics). Furthermore, the electron's motion is not continuous when it changes orbits; it's a discontinuous leap, a quantum jump (see figure 8, page 24).

How radical is the idea of the quantum leap! A quantum leap is like a jump from one rung of a ladder to another without going through the intervening space, something that nobody has ever seen. In order to recognize the existence of such quantum leaps in the atom, Bohr needed a discontinuous leap of his own—a shift of context in his understanding of physics, a turning from blind reliance on Newton's laws that posited continuity of motion to new quantum laws that had yet to be discovered. This is a classic example of fundamental creativity.

When Bohr finished his paper on his radical new discovery, he sent it to Rutherford in England as part of the process of publication. But Rutherford had difficulty appreciating Bohr's breakthrough. Bohr had to travel to England and convince Rutherford in person. It is said that when the physicist George Gamow brought Bohr's work to Einstein's attention, Einstein's eyes sparkled with excitement as he saw immediately that Bohr's discovery would make history as one of science's greatest accomplishments!

Situational Creativity

As an example of situational creativity, consider how the perception of a direct analogy enabled Alexander Graham Bell to invent the telephone. Here's what Bell wrote about his invention: It struck me that the bones of the human ear were very massive, as compared with the delicate thin membranes that operated them, and the thought occurred that if a membrane so delicate could move bones relatively so massive, why should not a thicker and stouter piece of membrane move my piece of steel . . . and the telephone was conceived.

Why did Bell succeed at inventing the telephone where so many had failed? What makes such people so special? What gives them their abilities to search the proper "problem spaces" of their mind (containing various known contexts), or their ability to identify and anticipate new meaning and value?

The point is that the particular mix of contexts, or the particular analogy leading to situational creativity cannot easily be anticipated from the existing contexts. That surprise occurs precisely because consciousness is seeing new meaning and value. It is conceivable that a computer might also be able to come up with the analogy Bell did by searching its problem spaces algorithmically. Computer programs can be good at fitting the problem to a previously known context that works. In the 1980s there was a program called *Soar* that, when given a new problem, searched first for an appropriate problem space. It then looked for a solution within that context. If it reached an impasse, it shifted to a new problem space, and so on, until it found the solution. There was no search for new meaning, however; all Soar's algorithms used symbols representing old meanings.

The famous U.K. engineer John Arnold agrees that in engineering all the preparation for an inventive project can be performed by a computer.[1] But when the computer comes up with a number of alternatives, the need for decision-making arises. Granted, a computer can calculate the probability of success of each of the alternatives, but, and this is Arnold's crucial point, the computer cannot assign values or meaning to the predictions, develop criteria for desirability, or judge archetypal truth or aesthetics. Said Arnold, "There is still ample opportunity and necessity for creative human work . . . in the stage of decision making."

Inner Creativity

As we've seen, an act of creativity is the exploration of new meaning that is of value in new and old context(s). Einstein's discovery of the theory of relativity revolutionized the way we consider time.

Before Einstein, we saw time as absolute, independent of everything else. After Einstein we had a new context for thinking about time: relativity. Time is elastic, depending on the velocity of observers, and time's relationship with space.

Suppose a student wants to learn Einstein's theory. It's very difficult and obscure at first, but at some point in her studies, understanding dawns. She has broken free from her old concept of time, and from this new perspective she can understand Einstein. Is this a creative act? Although there is no discovery or invention of a new meaning of context in the outer arena, no outer product, there is understanding of new meaning in the *inner* arena. Certainly far less creativity is needed to understand something like relativity than to discover it, or to apply it meaningfully in a new context. And yet she has discovered a new context of thinking about time for herself, and that surely has value; for her this is a creative act.

Indeed, I was such a student, and my pursuit of physics was the result of that first glimpse of the meaning of relativity. Similarly, when we read about people like Mahatma Gandhi, Martin Luther King, or Eleanor Roosevelt, we recognize that such people discovered ways to serve humanity that escape many of us. Yet the change of context they discovered was largely personal. Does that also qualify as creativity?

Yeshe Tsogyal, consort of the 8th-century mystic Padmasambhava, played a crucial role in the founding of Buddhism in Tibet. At one point in her life she was raped by a gang of bandits, who later became her disciples. What makes it possible for a person to so radically transform cruelty? The world's civilizations are greatly indebted to people such as Tsogyal, Buddha, Lao Tzu, Moses, Jesus, Muhammad, Shankara, and the like who found, lived, and communicated spiritual values to all humanity. Are their discoveries creative acts?

And what about the people who follow the spiritual paths laid out by these masters, often elucidating the path through their own work and dedication? Do their acts count as creativity?

Finally, what about people in ordinary life who discover and live unselfish love in relation with other people and the world? Do their discoveries amount to creativity?

The affirmative answer to all these questions leads us to see that creative acts fall into two broad categories that I call outer and inner creativity. Outer creativity yields objective products in the larger world. Inner creativity involves transformation of the self, and yields a subjective yet still-discernible product. Abraham Maslow, whose famous theory of positive psychological health was based on fulfilling certain internal needs, recognized the importance of inner creativity, which he called self-actualizing creativity; outer creativity he called talent-driven creativity.

Acts of outer creativity are usually judged in the context of what already exists. A new context is added to existing contexts (as we saw in Einstein's discovery of relativity). Although outer creativity is not restricted to geniuses, the arena of outer creativity is certainly dominated by people we now see as great men and women. Inner creativity, in contrast, is about a transformation of the individual self that yields new personal contexts of experiencing and living. It is evaluated in comparison not with others but with one's own old self. Here also there are great exemplars (like Buddha, Jesus, Moses, Mohammed, Shankara, and so on). But ordinary people also display inner creativity in their learning, understanding, and in the new and expanded contexts of their personal lives. The contributions to inner creativity of such unsung heroes form the backbone of human civilization.

So far we have been discussing inner creativity at the fundamental level. Transformation of the individual context of living (that we can recognize through a person's behavior) occurs only with people of fundamental creativity; their spiritual insights and life experiences help them define a "spiritual path." The popularization and explication of these paths constitute situational creativity. This is how the bulk of the knowledge systems of the great religions and ethical and moral systems of the world have been created.

To summarize, the phenomenon of creativity manifests in a four-fold classification scheme (figure 14). When you realize this vast scope of creativity, it's both humbling and inspiring, isn't it?

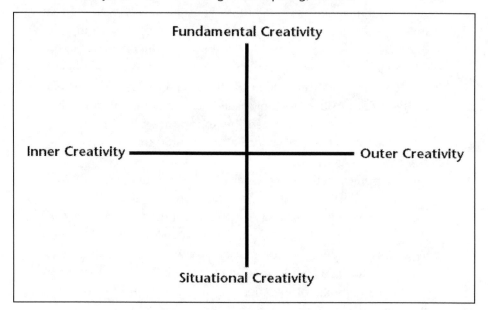

Figure 14: The four-fold classification of creativity

What is creativity?
The making of something new, we all agree.
If what you originate
Newly combines already known elements,
Then, oh creator, call your creativity situational.

Only if the flower of your creation
Blooms in a new context, as well,
And reflects new archetypal value
Is your creativity fundamental.

You can display the product
Of your outer creativity
Like a sun-illumined blossom on the bush.
Its perfume you share with others.

But you are the blossom
That opens from inner creativity.

Have you meditated, accepted the inner invitation?
Follow the trail of transformation.
Then only, oh creative, you share your being.

CHAPTER 5

Where Do Values Come From?

Creative acts are discontinuous. Here you are, stuck in already established meanings and contexts, and suddenly—bingo, eureka, aha! You've discovered a transcendent truth of great beauty. But where was your mind in between the old and new contexts? Let's take a look at some metaphors for the creative journey.

The English romantic poet Samuel Taylor Coleridge was quite graphic in describing his own creative journey and its symbols upon waking from a dream. "What if you slept," wrote Coleridge, "and what if in your sleep you dreamed? And what if in your dream you went to heaven and there plucked a strange and beautiful flower? And what if, when you awoke, you had the flower in your hand?" And Coleridge did! His heavenly flower found expression as his famous poem "Kubla Khan."

The following creation myth comes from a Native American tribe of California:

Everything was water except a very small piece of ground. On this were the eagle and coyote. Then the turtle swam to them. They sent it to dive for the earth at the bottom of the water. The turtle barely succeeded in reaching the bottom and touching it with its foot. When it came up again, all the earth seemed washed out. Coyote looked closely at its nails. At last he found a grain of earth. Then he and the eagle took this and laid it down. From it they made the earth as large as it is.[1]

These Native Americans saw the act of creation as diving deep into the ocean—another world—to find a grain of new "earth" (a new meaning of value) from which to build. It is the same with us. Like Coleridge's dream and the creation myth above, our creative acts come from a special domain of transcendent potentiality—the supramental land of the archetype into which we dive in our imagination to mine the hidden treasures of quantum consciousness. As we plunge into that unknown world we encounter precious formless entities. These are archetypal themes that have value—the contexts that form the essence of creative work. As we bring them back, the formless archetype takes on a new shape; bells ring, joy reverberates, and a creative act of discovery is born.

Our evolution so far has produced a brain that can at least seek to map the mind, but alas, we have no way to make direct physical representations of the supramental archetypes. Mental maps of them are the best we can do. Since there is no direct memory of our archetypal experiences, these experiences never get conditioned through memory. In other words, all supramental/archetypal experiences are quantum experiences of the self. And the quantum self is no stranger to us; every time we have an intuition (one kind of supramental experience), it is a beckoning of the quantum self. So as creative people we learn to value our intuitions.

The Archetype of Truth

One of our most important values is truth. All acts of fundamental creativity are in some way attempts to express some transcendent truth—which is also a common aspect of an archetype. "My country is truth," said the poet Emily Dickinson. Confusion arises when what a poet or artist portrays looks nothing like what we ordinarily call truth. The face of the artist's truth shifts from context to context; it is, as the Russian painter Wassily Kandinsky said, "constantly moving in slow motion." This is because the "whole" truth is transcendent; no perfect description of it here, in this world, is possible, as the novelist Hermann Hesse reminds us in these lines from *Siddhartha:*

Everything that is thought and expressed in words is one-sided, only half truth; it all lacks totality, completeness, unity. When the illustrious Buddha taught about the world, he had to divide it into Sansara and Nirvana, into illusion and truth, into suffering and salvation. One cannot do otherwise, there is no other method for those who teach. But the world itself, being in and around us, is never one-sided. Never is a man or deed wholly Sansara or Nirvana.[2]

Reality consists of both Nirvana and Sansara, both the transcendent (potential) and the immanent (manifest); our creativity attempts to express the transcendent in manifest form, but it never quite succeeds. A television character, trying to explain his garbled statement, once said, "You should have heard it before I said it." Strangely, he had a point. Expression compromises truth. Even our scientific laws do not express perfect archetypal truth, the whole truth. Science progresses when old laws yield to new ones as better theory and new data emerge, ever extending the domains of science.

Knowing that one of the goals of creativity is to make transcendent truth manifest (however imperfectly), we can understand the emphasis on a creative act that yields a tangible product. This product enables the creator to share the discovered truth with the external world, which is usually part and parcel of the creative undertaking. This is true of inner creativity as well. Gandhi said, "My life is my message."

Keeping in mind the idea of truth-value for an act of creativity, we begin to understand how we judge one particular act to be creative, and not another. Creative acts are those in which we sense a truth-value, where the archetypal themes are well represented, although in some cases (as in the case of Copernicus's heliocentric system or van Gogh's great impressionist art), this recognition of truth-value may take a long time.

Sometimes a particular artist is so successful in depicting an archetypal theme, the truth-value of his or her creative expression so authentic, that the art becomes immortal. Shakespeare's plays touch us even today (as they will millennia hence) because of his masterful exploration of archetypal themes. "Truth is that which touches the heart," said the novelist William Faulkner. Was he thinking of

Shakespeare? Othello's jealousy, Shylock's greed, and Macbeth's lust for power all come to life for us on stage today because we feel alive to the truth of the emotions they generate. Compare this to typical entertainment put out by the publishing, movie, and music industries every year; they don't lack in archetypes, perhaps, but they lack in truth-value, and very few of them sell well for long.

Beauty

Creative truth may not come with perfection, but it does come with beauty. The poet John Keats said, "Truth is beauty, beauty truth." Another poet, Rabindranath Tagore, wrote, "Beauty is truth's smile when she beholds her own face in a perfect mirror." If the authenticity of a creative insight cannot quite be judged by its truth-value, which is certain to be relative, at least it can be judged by its beauty.

Physicist Paul Dirac, one of the early architects of quantum physics, discovered a mathematical equation that predicts the existence of antimatter, material stuff that annihilates regular matter on contact. At the time, there was no reason to believe that such a thing existed, but Dirac was guided by a keen sense of aesthetics. As he put it, "It seems that if one is working from the point of view of getting beauty in one's equations, and if one has really a sound insight, one is on a sure line of progress." Indeed, Dirac's prediction came true a few years later in the form of the discovery of antiparticles. (True antimatter has been isolated only recently using CERN's supercollider machine.)

A legend about the medieval Bengali poet Jayadeva makes a similar point. Jayadeva was in the middle of creating a scene in his masterpiece *Gita Govinda,* in which "God-incarnate" Krishna is trying to appease his angry consort, Radha. An inspired line of great beauty came to the poet's mind, and he wrote it down. But then he had second thoughts: *Krishna is God incarnate; how could Krishna say such a human thing?* So he crossed the line out and went for a walk. According to the legend, while the poet was gone Krishna himself came and resurrected the line.

Throughout history humankind has recognized the power of beauty in creative acts. But what is beauty? Who judges it? Some authors try to find intellectual, emotional, or sociocultural causes for the aesthetic experience; some say beauty is experienced intellectually by seeing order and harmony where chaos would otherwise hold sway. Yet it is a truism that beauty is in the eyes of the beholder, the creative person. Dirac put it well when he said, "Well—you feel it. Just like beauty in a picture or beauty in music. You can't describe it, it's something—and if you don't feel it, you just have to accept you are not susceptible to it. No one can explain it to you."

When Pythagoras defined beauty as "the reduction of many to one," he was speaking of a very personal, transcendent experience. The poet Kahlil Gibran said the same thing:

> And beauty is not a need but an ecstasy
> It is not a mouth thirsting
> Nor an empty hand stretched forth,
> But rather a heart enflamed and a soul enchanted.
> It is not the image you would see nor the
> Song you would hear,
> But rather an image you see though you
> Close your eyes and a song you hear though
> You shut your ears.
> It is not the sap within the furrowed bark,
> Nor a wing attached to a claw,
> But rather a garden for ever in bloom and
> A flock of angels for ever in flight.[3]

The Many Splendors of Love

Love (and the Jungian Lover) is another important archetype. It is especially popular with poets, novelists, artists, and musicians. Love is also a path that people follow for spiritual growth. In others words, love is a many-splendored thing.

Love is a special archetype because its first representations were made in our physical body through the intermediary of the vital body long before we had the brain and the capacity for making mental representation. I am talking about the heart chakra, where according to the Hindu metaphysical system and other traditions we experience the feeling of romantic love. This is because the major heart chakra organ, the thymus gland, which is a part of the immune system, is a representation of the vital energies of romantic love. But this requires a little explanation.

Following highly original ideas of the maverick biologist Rupert Sheldrake, I see the vital—or energetic—body in terms of blueprints of biological functions called morphogenetic fields, which conscious-ness uses to make organs that perform those biological functions. This idea is shown in figure 15. The chakras are those points in our physical body where consciousness collapses both the organ and its correlated morphogenetic field. The energy we feel at a chakra comes from this vital field.

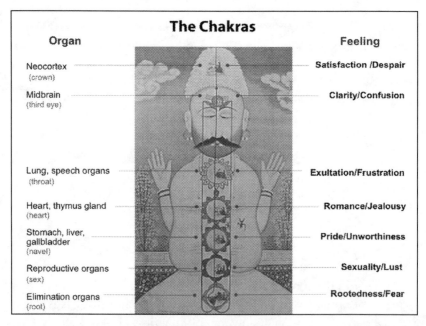

The Chakras

Organ	Feeling
Neocortex (crown)	Satisfaction /Despair
Midbrain (third eye)	Clarity/Confusion
Lung, speech organs (throat)	Exultation/Frustration
Heart, thymus gland (heart)	Romance/Jealousy
Stomach, liver, gallbladder (navel)	Pride/Unworthiness
Reproductive organs (sex)	Sexuality/Lust
Elimination organs (root)	Rootedness/Fear

Figure 15: The chakras. Archetypal biological functions descend to form via the inter-mediary of the morphogenetic fields; at the chakra point, consciousness simultane-ously collapses the biological organ at the chakra as well as the morphogenetic field that is represented by the organ. Creativity comes with affects because of associated movement of vital energy at the chakras.

To the right of the figure, you can see the different feelings that we experience at each chakra. The positive feelings associated with human creative experiences such as love, exultation, clarity, and satisfaction have their origin in the activation of the higher chakras (heart, throat, brow, and crown respectively). The negative feelings of fear, sexuality, and inadequacy and frustration are associated with the lower chakras (the root, sex, and the navel respectively).

The job of the immune system is to distinguish between "me" and "not me." If that distinction dissolves between two people, obviously the feeling would be "you are mine and I am yours"; in other words, romantic love. In this way, romantic love is really an agreement between the immune systems (and their associated morphogenetic fields) of the two lovers. The second chakra is a representation of sexual energy and this and the heart energy of romantic love are obviously connected. When we first become active in the second chakra in our adolescence, our tendency is to use sex to foster ego power. But if we wait for that special partner we can use sex for making love, and if we become committed to a romantic love partner, we can use this relationship for further exploration of the archetype of the lover.

Mind gives meaning to all our experiences, including romantic love. Our initial representations of the archetype of the lover are much influenced by our psychosocial conditioning. It takes creativity to discover the deeper meanings of love.

Ethics, Creativity, and the Archetypes of Goodness and Justice

Ethics, the form of philosophy that seeks to discriminate between good and evil, has been a serious concern of humankind from ancient times. Generally, the ethical prescription offered by most religious systems boils down to this: Do good unto others. The problem here is that it is not always easy to figure out what "good" is. The definition depends on the circumstances, which means that virtue will require situational creativity on our part, at the very least. At the very best, discovering a virtue to live by is a hero's journey. When we realize that the hero is really an archetype for which we can only make mental representations—that cannot be complete—we find support for the idea that there is always the need for creativity in our search for ethics to live by, both personal and social.

Along with the archetype of the hero, social ethics must also serve the archetype of the wise old man: everyone should have the opportunity to explore and fulfill their human potential for knowledge. The democracy that took hold in some parts of the world in the 18th century serves as a good example of creativity in the service of the hero and the wise old man. Unfortunately, some parts of the world have yet to catch up. The political movements in parts of the Middle East, known as the "Arab Spring," are a good start, but many more acts of creativity on behalf of freedom will be needed before democracy arrives in that part of the world.

One reason we have fallen behind in manifesting justice even in democracies is that we try to do it through laws aimed at problem solving, instead of being truly creative. In America today, through such movements as Occupy Wall Street, justice demands that everyone should have the opportunity to fulfill the American dream. This may seem impossibly idealistic until you realize that "human potential" and the "American dream" have to be defined not only in terms of material comfort but also in terms of meaning. This new definition of abundance will require a new economics and therefore much creativity in itself.

The Importance of Value Education

As we're beginning to see, fundamental creativity depends on our willingness to explore the archetypes, on our curiosity about them. Today, for example, lots of people, educators and politicians alike, talk about problems with our educational system. But seldom have I seen any clarity in these discussions about the root cause: the absence of an effort to teach values, particularly archetypal values such as truth, to our students. Just know that if a society undermines the timeless value of truth, it gets on Fox News. True, students can still draw on their intuition, but even this inherent gift needs to be reinforced and nurtured through education.

In the time before scientific materialism made such inroads in our society, we in America received value education from our religions, in such places as Sunday schools. But today this is much less prevalent. Although a majority of our people and our politicians (especially Republicans) still emphasize values, this is largely lip service. People, politicians specially, don't often walk their talk, and as a result most of us have become cynical. What if scientific materialism is right, and there are no values! What if archetypes are just flights of Plato's and Jung's imagination!

There is a lot of emphasis today on science and math education, but if we do not value the archetype of the sage, why should we engage in science and math—the foremost among our truth-seeking enterprises? Similarly, if we do not value such Platonic ideals as beauty or love, art loses its appeal. Can we engage in creativity—all that perspiration and agony—just for money and status? Money is a symbol; it has to represent something. There is nothing wrong with a monetary reward for our creative acts, but when money becomes the motive, we're no longer pursuing the real thing.

Materialism has led to our culture's worship of celebrity. Are famous people always creative? No, indeed. Fortunately, there are people who still follow archetypes and become famous anyway. Unfortunately, we still think fame is a sufficient motive for creativity. It never is and it never will be.

The lack of innovation in our society is solidly rooted in the absence of value education early on. Since religions have become ineffective as value educators, we have to do that job in our schools. Some religious people will see a red flag here—secularism. Relax. As science and spirituality become integrated, we must realize that value-archetypes are part of the self, they are not the exclusive province of religious creeds. Then we can move on to a post-secularism of value-oriented education.

But where can we find qualified teachers to teach values if we no longer turn to religion? The question reminds me of a story. A clergyman goes to heaven and St. Peter keeps him waiting at the pearly gate. "Look, an important fellow is coming, let him be received first, then we will take care of you," says he.

Soon the other person arrives. He's quite ordinary looking, but he's greeted with much fanfare. Afterward, St. Peter looks at our waiting clergyman and says kindly, "Now it's your turn." The priest is a little irritated by all the waiting, but he's also curious. He says, "Thank you. But can you tell me who that guy is? Why all the fuss?"

"Oh, he's a New York City taxi driver," says St. Peter.

The clergyman is dumbfounded. "What? You kept me waiting for a cab driver? After I devoted my entire life to the service of the Lord?"

St. Peter chuckles. "Yes, but when you preached people fell asleep. When he drove people in his taxicab, they prayed."

Does Creativity Have a Dark Side?

There is an important debate going on right now: Is there a dark side to creativity? Inventing the atomic bomb was a great scientific feat, no doubt about it. There is also no doubt that it was used to wreak terrible devastation on a huge number of innocent civilians. The discovery that there is immense energy locked in the atom's nucleus—certainly an example of fundamental creativity—can be blamed for all the evil it unleashed. So it certainly seems that there is a dark side to creativity.

It seems shocking at first when we look at this from a primacy-of-consciousness point of view. If creativity is a gift of nonlocal quantum consciousness, or what some refer to as God, how can the source of life and love be responsible for such dark acts? Why do bad things happen to good people? If God is perfect, why does evil exist?

One answer to these questions is evolution. Nonlocal consciousness uses downward causation to make new representations of its subtler and subtler possibilities in the manifest material world. Initially these representations are not perfect; matter is not ready yet. Hence the role of evolution. Evolution has to battle against the tendency for conditioned stasis. Often this requires violent uprooting that may look like acts of evil. So evil exists in the world so long as there is need for evolution. Nonlocal quantum consciousness itself is objective.

More insight into the question of evolution emerges when we look at the fact that when we manifest the product of our creativity we are very much in our ego. So sometimes our creative products bring more harm than good. Better days are ahead because evolution is progressive, and less and less violence will be needed to provide the impetus necessary to overcome stasis. As for our own role in the dark side of creativity, the remedy has been given by the spiritual traditions of the world for millennia. We can transform ourselves.

An Encounter with a Problem Solver

I was a little nervous when Dr. John Problemsolver showed up on my doorstep. John never shows up anywhere unless there's something that needs fixing. He seemed to read my mind.

"You're wondering what the problem is that I came here to solve. This time it is you, my friend; you are the problem," he said gravely, tossing his hat on a chair as he strode in.

I was surprised. "Now what have I done?"

"There is a rumor going around that you are reviving the notion that creativity is God's gift to us. What's worse is that you are using science to justify this preposterous notion."

"Read my book," I said, trying to conciliate him. "I haven't mentioned God much; I use the phrase 'quantum consciousness' instead."

"I know, I know," Problemsolver said impatiently. "I've read it. But you're using concepts like 'the unconscious,' which turn neurology into voodoo. What's more you are also using Sanskrit names—more voodoo. *Atman* brings us the creative insight from God, you say. Smacks of religion—specifically Hinduism, doesn't it?"

"Atman is our quantum self, our inner self, an identity taken by consciousness when a creative quantum measurement takes place in the brain. Atman doesn't come with Hinduism attached. No need to worry."

John did not seem conciliated. "Creativity is just problem solving, nothing more. Believe me, I know. I have never done any unconscious processing nor have I ever met any atman or quantum self, inside me or in the outside world. It is I who do all the work. Why should I give credit to the atman?"

"Well, you have a point. Indeed, atman isn't involved if you stay at the level of reasoning. Our continuous, local, thinking self is enough for that. But to quote the novelist Marcel Proust, 'A book is the product of a different self from the self we manifest in our habits, in our social life, in our vices.' When Einstein discovers the theory of relativity, or T. S. Eliot writes *The Waste Land,* surely they are not solving a situational problem, working within the dictates of reason. They're dancing to a different drummer altogether. I'm saying that in their case the drummer is the quantum self. Their creativity consists of making discontinuous quantum leaps into a nonlocal domain of pure potentiality—the supramental realm that is not accessible to the thinking ego. Creativity requires an encounter with the quantum self."

"You still don't get it," Problemsolver growled. "Einstein and Eliot are more talented than you or I, so they take on more difficult problems. But they're still problem-solving."

"Are they? When Einstein started his research, he didn't even know that the problem was the nature of time. He was worried about the nature of light. He was focusing on the compatibility of Newton's laws of mechanical movement with the theory of electricity and magnetism that Clerk Maxwell synthesized."

"Everybody knows that some people have to find their problem in order to solve it. Look, it makes sense. Einstein had a full-time job as a patent clerk. He couldn't devote a lot of time to physics so he looked for a problem that nobody else would be working on. It was just a strategic choice, simple survival instinct. And don't talk to me about T. S. Eliot. Poets are more than a little peculiar."

"Okay, let's stick to Einstein. You know, he once said something to the effect that 'I didn't discover relativity by rational thinking alone.' Einstein himself felt that he was doing something beyond rational thinking."

"Look, Einstein may have been some sort of mystic, so forget about him. Let's take a more recent example of creativity: Alexander Calder's mobile sculpture. We can trace his development of the abstract moving mobile down to that last detail. Turns out it's nothing more than solving the Charlie problem."

"What's that?"

"You don't know about the Charlie problem?" John sounded pleased to show off his expertise. "Dan comes home from work and finds Charlie lying dead on the floor. Tom's in the room, too, and on the floor Dan sees some water and broken glass. After taking one look at the situation Dan immediately knows how Charlie died. Do you?"

"I don't have the slightest idea. You know I'm not good at puzzles."

"Why don't you get your quantum self to help you? Oh, I know, I know. The quantum self won't dirty its hands with such trivia. So, do you want to know the answer?"

"Sure."

"When people try to solve the puzzle they assume that Charlie is a human being. But after being stuck for a while, they eventually question that assumption. And when they do—or when they ask for a clue and are told that Charlie wasn't human, they immediately figure out the answer."

"Aha! Charlie was a fish." I couldn't resist.

"See," Problemsolver said proudly, *"that's* how creativity works. You reach an impasse and you ask a new question. The answer makes you shift contexts, or combine old contexts, or transfer part of one context to another. Calder was already working on moving sculptures, regular forms that moved mechanically; maybe he got bored and was looking to do something different.

"So one day he visits an art gallery that's displaying the abstract art of Piet Mondrian. Immediately he thinks of using abstract pieces in his moving sculpture. You might call this a discontinuity, but the source of his shift of context was external—what he saw in the art gallery. Eventually Calder found that his mechanically driven abstract sculpture was also becoming boring. How to make it more interesting? This time he thought of chucking the mechanical movement and using wind to move his abstract forms. Not boring."

"That's a pretty good construction of Calder's creativity," I said, "but there's something missing in your equation.[4] Calder is a human being with ego; he has a belief system, and a way of doing things that identifies him professionally. Why should he change that just because he saw somebody's abstract art? You're a scientist who happens to believe that every phenomenon is a material phenomenon. You know that I think otherwise; I believe that every phenomenon is a phenomenon of consciousness. Let me ask you a question: Why don't you change your view of science after reading my work?"

"Well, I would have to understand and agree with your view first," said Problemsolver.

"Exactly. You have to explore new meaning. You have to explore the archetypes again to see the need for a new representation that intuition is hinting at. In this exploration, you touch the quantum self. This is what Calder did when he saw Mondrian's abstract art. Calder had a sudden inspired thought—a turnabout, a discontinuous shift from his past thinking on sculpture—when he explored the meaning of abstract art. He saw the possibility of representation in an entirely new way.

"Before this he had always thought of sculptures as straightforward representations of things in the world, something that makes sense, a recognizable form. In a sudden flash of inspiration he discovered the beauty of ambiguity that abstract painting represents, and he realized that he needed this ambiguity in his sculpture in order to bring his message—the transcendent beauty of moving forms—to people who saw his work.

"But even this did not satisfy him. The reliance on a mechanical device made his art too predictable. So he continued his search for a new context. Another day, after another encounter with the quantum self, he was inspired to replace motors with the whimsical movement of the wind. Now he had achieved not only ambiguity in form, but also ambiguity in movement itself, which is unusual in modern life."

"Now *that* is a tall tale if I ever heard one. So how does this encounter with the quantum self work?"

"You really want to know?" I replied, not a little pleased.

"I guess not. I might succumb to its influence. Then I wouldn't be satisfied with solving problems using my rational mind. But I hate to chase fundamental problems; they're too deep. And I don't believe in intuition. And chasing meaning is like pursuing a ghost. If all that wasn't difficult enough, I'm also not convinced there's any money in it."

With that John Problemsolver picked up his hat and left.

Creativity dwells not
In analysis and comparison.
Its abode is the twilight zone
Beyond locality.

There emperors and beggars,
Creatives, critics, and ordinary people
Bathe in the same shower of archetypal themes.
Consciousness moves,
And the quantum catapult of creativity
Launches us from the known to the unknown
And back again. From unconscious darkness
Comes the light of awareness.

Intuition transports us on quantum wings
Into the stream of that movement.

We enter a painting
Lose ourselves in music
Feel the keen joy or pain of a poem
Recognize ourselves in a story
See truth in a scientific law
Because an archetype of truth and beauty
Vibrates in our heart.
We have drunk from the same
Archetypal nectar as the creative!

PART II

THE CREATIVE PROCESS

CHAPTER 6

The Four Stages of the Creative Process

In dealing with the wholeness of the act of creativity, we must note not only what is discontinuous and extraordinary (the quantum leaps) but also what seems to be continuous and mundane. Charles Darwin's autobiography describes a creative moment of insight when, while reading Malthus's "Essay on Population," Darwin came to recognize the crucial role of fecundity in the theory of natural selection in biological evolution: The fact that species producing multiple offspring to replace themselves would quickly lead to an overpopulated planet were it not for limited resources, which means that individuals compete with each other for those limited resources. But according to creativity researcher Howard Gruber, a study of Darwin's notebooks shows that, while this was the final moment of insight, it was part of a gradual process interspersed with many smaller insights.

Of what does the entire creative process consist, then? Researcher Graham Wallas was one of the first to suggest that creative acts involve four stages, a view that is now commonly accepted.[1] These four stages are: preparation; incubation; sudden insight; and manifestation. Let's take a closer look at them now, and in the chapters that follow.

- **Stage 1: Preparation.** Gather facts and existing ideas about your problem and think, think, think. Talk with experts; attend workshops. Churn your ideas, looking at them in every way that comes to mind. Give your imagination free rein.

- **Stage 2: Incubation.** The problem is not going away, so while it's percolating in your mind, you can play, sleep, and do things that relax you. (Include especially bath, bus, and apple tree—they have demonstrated relevance: Archimedes made his "Eureka" discovery while taking a bath; the mathematician Henri Poincaré had a major insight while boarding a bus; and Newton discovered gravity while sitting under an apple tree.)

- **Stage 3: Sudden insight.** Eureka! Right when you least expect it, illumination dawns. The surprise of this moment is a hallmark of discontinuity.

- **Stage 4: Manifestation.** The fun is over—or is it just beginning? Verify, evaluate, and manifest what you've come up with. In other words, make a product of your insight.

Preparation begins with an intuition, a vague feeling about the answer to a possible problem. There is a question, a curiosity at work, but it's not burning. However, as you keep doing the relevant ground-work—gathering information, asking questions about the existing structure, and so forth—your curiosity takes on a growing intensity. When you get well acquainted with the field and yet the feeling per-sists that you are on the verge of a discovery, urgency appears; the questions begin to nag at you as the dismantling of existing belief system(s) begins to take place.

At this point, says psychologist Carl Rogers, your mind becomes open, setting the stage for unbridled possibilities and acceptance of the new.[2] We can see a good example of the importance of an open mind in 17th-century physicist Johannes Kepler, who came up with the revolutionary idea that the planets in our solar system move in ellipses around the sun. Long before Kepler's final insight, he had logi-cally considered the possibility of the ellipse as an option for planetary orbits, but had discarded the idea as a "cartload of dung." He was not yet prepared for the new. He lacked an open mind—until he didn't.

Wallas and many other researchers believe that incubation involves unconscious mental processing. Quantum physics gives us an explanation: Unconscious processing is quantum processing—it takes place in the nonlocal realm of many possibilities at once. When Niels Bohr was working on his model of the atom, he saw the solar system in a dream, suggesting unconscious incubation in his psyche. Behaviorally, we can equate incubation with relaxation—"sitting quietly, doing nothing"—as opposed to preparation, which is active work.

The third stage, where discontinuity enters, is of course, the most spectacular. The transition from unconscious possibilities to conscious insight, from stage two to stage three, requires downward causation, which acts discontinuously.

Finally, manifestation involves working with the insight, checking the solution, and ending up with a product—the manifest novelty. With manifestation comes a restructuring of the belief system, or at least an extension of the repertoire of learned contexts. In this way it is like the dance of Shiva, the destroyer and creator in Hindu mythology (figure 16).

Figure 16: Shiva's dance. In one hand he holds the drum to announce creation; in the other he holds the fire of destruction. The dwarf under his feet represents ignorance. Altogether a wonderful metaphor for the creative act.

Could the brain do all this on its own, as materialists claim? No materialist model can distinguish unconscious from conscious; the neurophysiology of experience (let alone creative experience) is a "hard" problem that is beyond the reach of scientific materialism to explain. Furthermore, brain-based explanations suffer from inconsistency. How does the brain search for meaning if it is a material machine, since matter cannot process meaning? How does the brain pull together "ideas" from different brain areas without nonlocal capacity? How does an idea "enter" consciousness if there is no distinction between conscious and unconscious? Face it. A brain-based explanation of creativity is a prime example of what is now called "fact-free" science. It's the same basis some conservatives provide for their regular denials of global climate change.

Preparation:
Gandhi spinning cotton on his wheel,
Preparing for *satyagraha*—
Readiness for truth.
Incubation:
Picasso at a sidewalk cafe in Paris
Sitting quietly, doing nothing.
Insight:
Amadeus, feverishly recording the notes of the *Requiem*,
Its music filling his mind space.
Manifestation:
Madame Curie, extracting a grain of radium
From a mountain of uranium.
When infinity plays my finite instrument—creation!
I tune my instrument and listen for the invitation to creativity.
Opto ergo sum.

CHAPTER 7

Is Creative Insight a Quantum Leap?

Creative ideas come to us, in physicist Nikola Tesla's phrase, "like a bolt of lightning." Creative thoughts that shift our contexts or reveal new meaning are discontinuous leaps from our ordinary stream-of-consciousness thoughts. Henri Poincaré pondered a mathematical problem for days, but nothing happened in his conscious, step-by-step thinking. But later, on a trip, a new context for mathematical functions came to him unexpectedly, discontinuously, as he was boarding a bus. He later reported the idea had no connection to his thoughts at the time, or to his previous thinking on the subject.

The king of Syracuse, in ancient Greece, wanted to find out if a certain crown was made of real gold, and who but his favorite scientist, Archimedes, could determine this without mutilating the crown? It is said that Archimedes suddenly hit upon the idea for an answer when he set foot in a full bathtub and the tub overflowed. So exalted was he that he ran naked in the streets of Syracuse shouting "Eureka! Eureka!" ("I found it! I found it!") The solution Archimedes discovered started a new branch of hydrostatics.

The mathematician Carl Friedrich Gauss provides an example of the discontinuity of a creative insight in this way:

> Finally, two days ago, I succeeded, not on account of my painful efforts, but by the grace of God. Like a sudden flash of

lightning, the riddle happened to be solved. I myself cannot say what was the conducting thread which connected what I previously knew with what made my success possible.[1]

Notice the insistence on the role of the "grace of God." This undoubtedly reflects Gauss's keen awareness that he did not make the discovery via step-by-step thinking.

The composer Brahms also saw the discontinuity of his insight as help from God. He described his creative experience composing his most famous music with these words:

> Straightaway the ideas flow in upon me, directly from God, and not only do I see distinct themes in my mind's eye, but they are clothed in the right forms, harmonies, and orchestration. Measure by measure the finished product is revealed to me when I am in those rare, inspired moods.[2]

Here is an equally compelling quote about the suddenness of creativity from the great composer, Tchaikovsky:

> Generally speaking, the germ of a future composition comes suddenly and unexpectedly. . . . It takes root with extraordinary force and rapidity, shoots up through the earth, puts forth branches and leaves, and finally blossoms. I cannot define the creative process in any way but [by] this simile.[3]

The English romantic poet P. B. Shelley expressed the discontinuity of writing poetry succinctly: "Poetry is not like reasoning, a power to be exerted according to the determination of the will. A man cannot say, 'I will write poetry.' The greatest poet even cannot say it."

Henry Wadsworth Longfellow puts his experience of discontinuity while writing a ballad in a somewhat different way:

> Last evening I sat till twelve o'clock by my fire, smoking, when suddenly it came into my mind to write the 'Ballad of the Schooner Hesperus,' which I accordingly did. Then I went to bed, but could not sleep. New thoughts were running in my mind, and I got up to add them to the ballad. I felt

pleased with the ballad. It hardly cost me any effort. It did not come into my mind by lines, but by stanzas.[4]

Note the words "not . . . by lines, but by stanzas." Not bit by bit, but as a whole, discontinuously. This wholeness is characteristic of the quantum nature of creative insights, and even when an idea is only part of a whole solution, it acts as a seed for the wholeness that follows.

There is also ample evidence of discontinuity in dream creativity. Chemist Dmitri Mendeleev, who discovered the famous periodic table of chemical elements, said, "I saw in a dream a table where all the elements fell into place as required." Mathematician Jacques Hadamard reported discovering the long-sought solutions of problems "at the very moment of sudden awakening [from dreams]." Beethoven wrote about finding a canon while in a dream:

> I dreamt that I had gone on a far journey, to no less a place than Syria, on to Judea and back, and then all the way to Arabia, when at length I arrived at Jerusalem. . . . Now during my dream journey, the following canon came into my head. . . . But scarcely did I awake when away flew the canon, and I could not recall any part of it. On returning here however, the next day . . . I resumed my dream journey, being on this occasion wide awake, when lo and behold! In accordance with the law of association of ideas, the same canon flashed across me; so being now awake I held it as fast as Menelaus did Proteus, only permitting it to be changed into three parts.[5]

Objective Data

From the objective standpoint of scientific materialism, subjective reports of discontinuous shifts in consciousness like those cited above are suspect as evidence for the discontinuity in creativity, but there is objective evidence, too, of such quantum leaps of creativity!

There is the phenomenon of quantum healing (spontaneous healing without medical intervention) that must be seen as a creative breakthrough, as the following case history shows.[6] A patient designated as

S.R. was diagnosed with Hodgkin's disease. S.R. was pregnant and did not want to lose the baby. So she refused chemotherapy and found a new doctor under whose supervision she had surgery, even radiation treatment, but the situation continued to get worse.

Her physician was researching LSD therapy for cancer. S.R. took a guided LSD trip during which the doctor encouraged her to go deep inside herself and communicate with the life in her womb. As S.R. did that, her physician asked if she had the right to cut off the new life. It was then that S.R. had the sudden flash of insight: She had the choice to live or die—a quantum leap. She chose life. It took a while after this insight, and a lot of lifestyle changes, but she was healed—quantum healing. You can deny the veracity of what she did or said, but the hard fact remains that she was healed without medical intervention. Incidentally, she also gave birth to a healthy child.

Thanks to Dr. Deepak Chopra and researchers at the Institute of Noetic Sciences in California, there is now much documented data of such quantum healing—spontaneous healing without medical intervention.[7] Another source of objective data in support of quantum leaps of creativity consists of the many fossil gaps that are found between otherwise continuous fossil lineages.[8]

There is also a source of suggestive support for the discontinuity of creativity. Mythology, said the philosopher William Irwin Thompson, is the history of the soul (consciousness). The importance of discontinuity in creative acts is immortalized in India by the Valmiki myth: Ratnakar was a hunter who once killed two birds who were making love. He became so moved after realizing what evil he had done that lines of poetry spontaneously came out of his mouth and he was transformed. Later he became known as Valmiki and wrote the great Indian epic of the *Ramayana.* In the West, very tellingly, there is the myth of Newton's apple—the falling of an apple is said to have triggered a discontinuous shift in Newton's discovery of gravity.

Discontinuity in Newton's Discovery of Gravity

It was 1665, and a plague had broken out in Cambridge, England. The University of Cambridge closed, and Isaac Newton, who was teaching at the university, moved to his mother's farm in Lincolnshire. There one day in the garden, Newton saw an apple fall to earth. This triggered in his consciousness a universal insight: every object attracts every other with the force of gravity.

What does the apple story mean to you or me? Apples fall every day, and hardly anyone notices. This was just as true in Newton's time as it is in ours. Indeed, according to many historians, the apple story is not fact but fancy, perhaps started by Newton's niece. So why does the apple story survive even in physics textbooks, side by side with scientific method? Because myths remind us of deeper truths.

It is not difficult to reconstruct Isaac Newton's discovery in a way that shows how logic must have led to his sudden insight. Before Newton, Johannes Kepler had proposed that planets revolve around the sun in nearly circular orbits. One of Newton's early goals was to find an explanation for Kepler's laws. Another of Newton's curiosities involved Galileo's work on bodies falling toward earth.

Newton himself formulated laws of motion that tie the accelerated motion of objects to the external forces acting on them. Newton must have recognized that the movement of planets around the sun, or of the moon around the earth, must be the result of an external force exerted by the sun on a planet, or of earth's attraction on the moon. The problem was that there was no such known force. Seeing the apple fall triggered in Newton's consciousness the creative insight that the two movements, the apple's and the moon's, owe their origin to a universal "gravitational" force that the earth exerted on each of them. Is that all there is to such a game-changing act of creativity? That doesn't sound like much, does it?

Hold on. We're forgetting something. According to the prevailing belief system at the time, earthly and heavenly laws were different; the Greeks told us so! Moreover, no force had ever been known to act at a distance without an intermediary. In suggesting that earth exerted a force called gravity on an apple, Newton was proposing the existence of a universal force: that any two objects interact this way regardless of their placement in space—on earth or in the heavens. Thus the physics that Newton's research unveiled was not to be found in known contexts. As the physicist Paul Dirac said, great ideas overcome great prejudices.

Gestalt

In psychology the word *gestalt* means the whole, the difference between an integrative pattern and a collection of separate fragments. Suddenly, discontinuously, the pattern clicks in the mind of the beholder, as when the gestalt of the young and the old woman in the same lines of Figure 4 (page 18) appears to you.

The perception of the gestalt can be seen in the realization of the harmony of a musical composer's pattern of notes. Mozart and Brahms have said that their music came to them as a whole theme, not with bit-by-bit continuity, and the romantic poet Samuel Coleridge said the same of his poem "Kubla Khan." You and I can get nearly the same pleasure by looking at some of M. C. Escher's drawings and suddenly recognizing the "wholeness" of the artist's pattern. In the throes of creativity, the scientist is no different from a musician or an artist. Many important creative discoveries are like this: all or nothing.

A dangerous prisoner's legs are injured in a machine shop accident. He is sent to the prison hospital, where he is closely guarded. Unfortunately for the prisoner, his left leg develops gangrene and has to be amputated; the prisoner insists that he be given the leg so that he can give it to a friend for proper disposal. When his friend visits, the prisoner gives him his leg while the guard looks on.

But the prisoner's condition continues to worsen, and his right leg, too, becomes gangrenous and has to be amputated. Again his friend comes to pick up the leg for proper disposal. Now the guard becomes suspicious. After the friend leaves, the guard confronts the prisoner. "What is all this, giving your legs to your friend? Are you trying to escape?" No prisoner ever has escaped piece by piece—it's all or nothing.

Isn't it a good thing that quantum creativity includes unconscious processing? In unconscious processing, no parts of the eventual gestalt are discarded prematurely, as they would be in conscious processing if they had no obvious utility.

The same reasoning is compelling for seeing why quantum creativity is essential for understanding biological evolution, especially the fast tempo of evolution that many biologists have proposed in order to explain the famous fossil gaps. Such evolution cannot possibly be explained by the slow bit-by-bit accumulation of gene mutations and selection by nature as Darwinism proposes. If we see gene mutations as a quantum process producing quantum possibilities, then we can easily see that mutations can accumulate in potential until the possibilities collapse into the gestalt necessary for producing an organ, and actualization can take place as a quantum leap.

Case History: Picasso's *Guernica*

Let's take a close look at Picasso's painting of *Guernica,* taking advantage of the fact that Picasso left notebooks that have stimulated comments by many researchers. Picasso was commissioned by the Spanish government to create a mural for Spain's exhibit at the Paris World Fair in 1937. Originally Picasso planned to paint a scene in an artist's studio, but after the Nazi bombing of Guernica, Picasso decided to portray the devastated town.

And what an impressive painting it is (figure 17). We recognize a horse and a bull, torn up and in agony. We see a mother grieving the dead child in her arms; a woman, lamp in hand, looking out the window of a burning building; a woman falling from another burning building, her clothes aflame as another woman runs into the scene.

The brutal effect of the bombing certainly comes through, but as great artists do, Picasso manages to convey much more. Picasso saw in the agony of the people of Guernica the pain of all living beings. It is no coincidence that the only male figure in the painting is a shattered statue of a warrior (that Picasso was inspired to add as the painting neared completion). The warrior represents the condition of the archetypal hero in this materialist age. Yes, *Guernica* is a portrait of our own fragmented psyche.

Figure 17: Picasso's *Guernica*

Art historians note ambiguity about whether the scene is exterior or interior. The woman leaning out a window suggests the former, but lines in the upper corner indicate the latter. Can that ambiguity be purposeful? As an exterior painting, it depicts the indiscriminate horrors of war. As an interior painting, it conveys the horrible fragmentation of our psyches. And in its depiction of a larger truth, *Guernica* transcends duality. The painting of *Guernica* was an act of fundamental creativity because, while painting it, Picasso took a local truth and made it global; by gaining access to the archetypal fabric of the universe he saw the future of humanity. In their discovery of new contexts, great artists often jump way ahead of their time—and are sometimes aware of doing so. Gertrude Stein, a contemporary of Picasso, once complained to him, "Your figures don't look much like human beings." But Picasso replied, "Don't worry, they will."

Understanding Discontinuity

In a delightful Sidney Harris cartoon (figure 18), Einstein, baggy pants and all, stands before a blackboard with chalk in hand, ready to discover a new law. On the board, the equation $E = ma^2$ is written and crossed out; under it $E = mb^2$ is also crossed out. The caption reads, "The Creative Moment." Why do we laugh at it? It's a marvelous caricature of a creative moment precisely because we all intuitively recognize that a creative insight involves discontinuity.

Figure 18: *The Creative Moment* (by Sidney Harris)

As a child, when I first learned to count up to a hundred, I did it because my mother drilled the numbers into me. She established the context, and I learned by rote; the numbers themselves had no meaning for me. Next I was told to consider sets of two and three: two pencils, two cows, three bananas, and three pennies. Then one day, all of a sudden, the difference between two and three (and all other numbers) became clear to me as I saw the concept of the set (without formally knowing it, of course). Although people in my environment, like my mother, facilitated my "getting" it, in the ulti-mate reckoning it was I who discovered the meaning. And it *was* like a bolt of lightning!

Researcher Gregory Bateson, with his definition of levels of learn-ing, offers further insight into the idea of a discontinuous shift of con-text in learning. According to Bateson, lower-level learning, which he called "Learning I," takes place within a given, fixed context; this is conditioned or rote learning. Learning II requires the ability to shift the context. To my way of thinking, Level II learning is creative learning requiring a quantum leap. It contributes to inner creativity. It may be facilitated by good teachers, but nobody can teach it to us. It takes place inside us.

Angst, Surprise, and Certainty (or Agony, Ecstasy, and the Shiver in the Spine)

If you look back at your own childhood, you will find ample evidence of discontinuity. Try this exercise. Close your eyes and remember when you had your first experience of 1) comprehending what you were reading, 2) understanding math, 3) executing a spontaneous dance step or bursting into song, 4) conceptualizing the context of a number, or 5) suddenly understanding a foreign language if you were living outside your own country. See what I mean?

The discontinuity of creative experiences reveals itself as a surprise, which is the reason they are sometimes called "aha" moments. There is also ecstasy associated with the successful leap to uncharted territory; the remarkable sense of wholeness in the quantum self-experience soothes the ego-anxiety of seeking without knowing what is sought (associated with the navel chakra).

The songwriter P. F. Sloan describes his agony, his struggles during the writing of a song, with these words, with which we all can relate: "I was up most of that night battling. I don't know who I was battling or what, but I vividly recall saying to some higher power, 'Please let me be released from this. Please let me get out. Let me be released.'"

But a voice kept telling him, "NO, no, sorry, you've got to live with it. Can't let you fall on this one."

And then the ecstasy. "Finally, the words would start to come and I would see them and I would be filled with tears of joy, and I would be so happy that they were being given."

Once again, believers in scientific objectivism see such personal experiences as subjective, and therefore unreliable. However, as we'll see in the following example of research with dolphins conducted by Gregory Bateson, there is an abundance of compelling objective evidence of discontinuity in learning.

A dolphin at the Oceanic Institute in Hawaii was taught to expect food at the sound of the trainer's whistle. Later, if she repeated whatever she was doing at the time the whistle blew, she would hear the whistle again and be given more food. This dolphin was used to demonstrate training techniques to the public, who were told by the trainer, "When she enters the exhibition tank, I'll watch her and when she does something I want her to repeat, I'll blow the whistle and she will be fed." In order to demonstrate this in repeated public performances, the trainer had to reward a different (new) behavior with the whistle and food at each new performance; this was a Learning I response. But every once in a while Bateson saw an entirely different kind of response:

> In the time out between the fourteenth and the fifteenth session, the dolphin appeared to be much excited; and when she came onstage for the fifteenth session, she put on an elaborate performance that included eight conspicuous pieces of behavior of which four were new and never before observed in this species of animal. From the animal's point of view, there is a jump, a discontinuity . . .[9]

In addition to ecstasy and surprise, the discontinuity of creativity comes with another telling characteristic: certainty. Do you remember an occasion when a sudden insight revealed the solution to a problem? Now compare the quality of your certainty on that occasion with a time when you relied only on reason, and you will see what I mean. Einstein, after his theory of general relativity was verified, was sitting on his desk with piles of congratulatory telegrams when a newswoman asked how he would feel if the experiment had not confirmed his theory. To that Einstein replied, "Then I would have felt sorry for the dear Lord. The theory is correct."

Some people report a telling characteristic felt during a creative thought—an unmistakable feeling of the movement of vital energy. Some people report this as a "shiver through the spine." Others say that their knees shake.

In sum, the world does not just operate deterministically, a captive to past conditioning. If you are free to act with quantum creativity, you have access to new possibilities at every moment.

A Cossack saw a rabbi walking toward the town square every day at about the same time. One day he asked, "Where are you going, rabbi?"

The rabbi replied, "I am not sure."

"You pass this way every day at this time. Surely, you know where you're going."

When the rabbi maintained that he didn't know, the Cossack became angry, then suspicious, and finally took the rabbi to jail. Just as he was locking the cell, the rabbi faced him and said gently, "Now you can see why I didn't know."

Before the Cossack intercepted him, the rabbi had an idea of where he was going, but he didn't *know;* the intervention—we might see it as a quantum measurement—changed the future progression of events. This is the message of the worldview based on quantum physics. The world is not determined by its initial conditions, once and for all; every event is potentially creative, bearing new possibilities.

> A creative thought is a quantum hit, no less,
> A quantum leap to new archetypal context or meaning.
> Babies do it, dolphins do it.
> Artists, poets, musicians, scientists—
> Quantum leapers all.
> They are not scared by discontinuity.
> Are you?

CHAPTER 8

The Evidence for Unconscious Processing

Although psychologist Sigmund Freud pioneered the idea of the unconscious as the repository of repressed material, and his protégé Carl Jung added the understanding of a collective unconscious, a repository of shared images and archetypes common to all humans, quantum physics gives us a more complete understanding of it. All quantum objects exist in two levels of reality: in the transcendent level objects exist as possibility in the realm of potentiality; in the immanent level, objects are made manifest. We have access to both realms. The transcendent potentiality we process in the unconscious state, where we have no subject-object split awareness. The immanent we experience with conscious awareness.

Freud and Jung cited dreams as evidence of unconscious processing of repressed material, and indeed there is considerable evidence of the unconscious in dreams. The case of pharmacologist Otto Loewi is interesting because his brilliant idea for demonstrating that nerve impulses are chemically mediated came from a dream, but with a quirk. The first time he dreamed it, he wrote the dream down when he awoke momentarily, but the following morning he could not decipher his own handwriting. Fortunately, the next night he dreamed the same idea again. This time he was careful to write it down legibly![1]

Carl Jung stressed the archetypal content of creative dreams.[2] In the experience of inventor Elias Howe we can see how the archetypal content of dreams can support the creative act. Howe was in the final stage of designing the first sewing machine, but he was stuck; he couldn't see a way for the needle and thread to work together. In a dream Howe was captured by savages whose leader demanded that he finish his invention or be executed. As he prepared to die, Howe noticed the unusual shape of his captors' spears; they had eye-shaped holes (a well-known archetypal image) near the points. Waking from the dream, Howe realized instantly that the key to making his sewing machine work was a needle with a hole near the point for thread.

Objective Evidence

To scientific materialists dreams don't count; they are too subjective to take seriously. However, objective scientific evidence of the unconscious is mounting. First, psychologist Nicholas Humphrey found a human subject with defects in his cortex that had caused him to become blind in the left visual field of both eyes. But the man could point to a light on his blind side with accuracy, and could also use blind sight to distinguish crosses from circles and horizontal lines from vertical ones. But when asked how he "saw" these things, the man insisted that he just guessed, in spite of the fact that his hit rate was far beyond mere chance. Cognitive scientists now agree that this phenomenon, known as blind sight, represents unconscious processing—processing optical stimuli without awareness.[3]

Secondly, research done on the brain's electrical responses to a variety of subliminal messages provides further physiological and cognitive evidence for unconscious processing. A meaningful picture (for example, a bee) flashed on a screen for a thousandth of a second elicits a stronger response than a more neutral picture (such as an abstract geometrical figure). Furthermore, when subjects were asked to free-associate after these subliminal exposures, they used words like *sting* and *honey*. Clearly, there must have been unconscious processing of the picture of the bee without awareness to elicit responses like "sting"!

Thirdly, cognitive experiments using words with multiple meanings support the distinction between the conscious and the unconscious mind. In conscious processing there is collapse and awareness—subject-object split. In unconscious processing, in which consciousness is present in the absence of awareness, there is no collapse of the possibility wave. In a representative experiment, cognitivist Anthony Marcel used strings of three words in which the middle word was ambiguously associated with the other two words; his subjects watched a screen as the three words were flashed one at a time at intervals of either 600 milliseconds or 1.5 seconds between flashings. The subjects were then asked to push a button when they consciously recognized the last word of the series.[4]

The original purpose of the experiment was to use the subject's reaction time as a measure of the relationship between congruence or lack of it among the words and the meanings assigned to the words in such series as *hand-palm-wrist* (congruent) and *tree-palm-wrist* (incongruent). For example, the bias of the word *hand* followed by the flashing of *palm* may be expected to produce the hand-related meaning of *palm*, which then should improve the reaction time of the subject for recognizing the third word, *wrist* (congruence). But if the biasing word is *tree*, the lexical meaning of *palm* as a tree would be assigned to the next word (so far so good), but the recognition of the third word, *wrist*, should take a longer reaction time because it is incongruous. And indeed, this was the result.

However, when the researchers masked the middle word by a pattern that made it impossible to see with awareness, though unconscious perception continued, there was no longer any appreciable difference in reaction time between the congruent and the incongruent cases. This is surprising because presumably both meanings of the ambiguous word were available, regardless of the biasing context, yet neither meaning was chosen over the other. Apparently, then, choice, and therefore quantum collapse, is a concomitant of conscious experience but not of unconscious processing.

The Marcel experiment directly demonstrates the existence of macroscopic superpositions of possibilities of thought-maps (macroscopic quantum states) in the brain. Before choice, in the quantum description, the ambiguous state of the brain subject to a pattern-masked, ambiguous-word stimulus is a superposition of two possible thought-maps.

Fourth, still more evidence for unconscious processing comes from research on split-brain patients whose cortical connections between the two hemispheres of the brain are severed, but whose hindbrain (associated with feelings and emotions) connections are intact. In one experiment, a woman was shown the picture of a nude male model in her left visual field (which connects to the right brain hemisphere). The woman blushed but could not explain why. Clearly, the unconscious processing involving the right brain and the hindbrain triggered a thought (and a feeling) without her being aware of a cause.

Finally, some remarkable data for unconscious processing has come to light in connection with near-death experiences. After a cardiac arrest some people literally die (as shown by a flat EEG reading), only to be revived through the marvels of modern cardiology. Some of these near-death survivors report viewing their own surgery as if they were hovering over the operation table, providing specific details that leave no doubt they are telling the truth.[5]

Even blind people report such remote vision during near-death coma, which suggests that they may be using nonlocal distant-viewing ability to access the eyes of others involved with the surgery: doctors, nurses, and so forth.[6] But how do these patients "see," even nonlocally, while they are technically dead, and therefore incapable of collapsing possibility waves? The explanation is that a chain of possibilities collapses retroactively in time, that a delayed collapse takes place at the moment of return of the brain function as noted by the EEG.

Can quantum collapse take place in a delayed fashion in response to our delayed choice? In 1993 researcher Helmut Schmidt recorded radioactive decay events, and with the help of Geiger counters and computers set the radioactive events up as a random array of zeroes and ones, which was then printed out and sealed in an envelope, without anyone having looked at any of the events leading up to that moment. After a few months, psychics tried to psychokinetically influence the radioactive decay in a particular chosen direction. They succeeded *even though months had elapsed since the original decay process.* Schmidt also found that if an observer, unbeknownst to everyone else, opened the sealed envelope and examined the printout beforehand, the data could not be influenced by any psychic maneuver. The conclusion is simple, straightforward, and astounding: quantum events remain in possibility until consciousness looks at and actualizes them—*even if that takes place after what we assume as the fact!*

Be patient and persistent.
Do.
Stoke the creative process
With your burning question.
But never ignore being.
When a flaming leap of context bursts forth,
The radiant answer takes you to Einstein's ecstasy.

CHAPTER 9

The Agony, the Aha, and the Ecstasy

"Creativity occurs in an act of encounter," said Rollo May, "and is to be understood with this encounter as its center."[1] Actually, it is more than that. An act of creativity is the fruit of the prolonged struggle between ego and quantum consciousness—the conscious processor of the old and the unconscious processor of the new, and also between the ego self and the quantum self. It is this latter "intersection of the childlike and the mature," to quote creativity researcher Howard Gardner, which manifests as the product others can see. Often the creator is unaware of the deeper, inner interplay of the conscious and the unconscious.

Who presides over the unconscious? In unconscious processing there is an ongoing struggle to shift from the authority of ego conditioning to the creative freedom of the quantum consciousness. For real freedom and creativity we have to surrender the unconscious to quantum consciousness; we do this by allowing the pool of possibilities to expand to contain the new, by inviting ambiguity in our waking life, for example. Michelangelo left us a wonderful archetypal image on the ceiling of the Sistine Chapel of the surrender of the ego to a God that it cannot quite touch (figure 19).

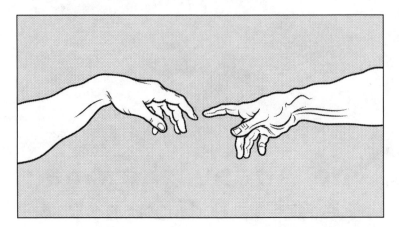

Figure 19: The creative interaction of God (quantum consciousness)
and the ego (Adam) as depicted by Michelangelo

One sign of the struggle is anxiety. Researchers have trained animals to discriminate between shapes, say a circle and an ellipse. But after the distinction is learned, the task is made progressively more difficult—the ellipse becomes rounder and rounder, looking more and more like the circle. Finally there is no difference at all, and discrimination is impossible. At this stage the animal begins to show symptoms of severe anxiety, whereas naive animals (those not taught to distinguish between an ellipse and a circle) do not exhibit this phenomenon of "experimental neurosis."

Why this neurosis? The smaller capacity of the animal's brain makes the animal unable to handle creative anxiety, unable to make room for the new. In contrast to these lower animals, the dolphin-training experiments we read about earlier demonstrate that dolphins are able to handle the anxiety of the creative struggle. This is because, like us, they are capable of a larger repertoire of learned programs, and thus they have a stronger, more secure, more developed ego.

In ordinary experience the ego is at the top of a simple hierarchy of mental programs, our learned representations of the world; in a creative flow experience, however, there is a discontinuity, an unexpectedness, and the possibility that the experience may not spring from the ego's learned repertoire. Researcher Keith Sawyer wrote about jazz performers that "many describe the experience of being surprised by what they play, or they discuss the importance of not being consciously in control," but the comment applies to all creative people who are in the flow.

Experiments conducted during surgery by neurophysiologist Benjamin Libet and his collaborators give us an idea of the time scale for the ego/quantum-self encounter. When Libet applied a stimulus to a patient's hand, the patient was able, in about 200 milliseconds, to press a button to indicate that the stimulus had reached his brain; but it took 500 milliseconds for the patient to report the touch using a verbal response.[2] The difference is the time taken for secondary-awareness processing—call it preconscious processing.

We have to gain access to the twilight zone of the preconscious and penetrate through the maze of memory playbacks and conditioned responses to join the swifter, unconditioned play of the quantum self. We gain entry to the preconscious when there is a creative encounter of the ego and the quantum self, and there is "flow," spontaneity of experience that contributes to the ecstasy of creativity. You very likely have experienced a few enchanted moments of flow when the ego ceases to be central. You may have had the feeling of "losing yourself" in music, or swimming, or artistic creation.[3] At such times we access two modes of experience: the quantum self, in which creative freedom and spontaneity overrule deliberation and past conditioning; and the ego, which contributes its expertise, its learned repertoire of past contexts with which to make representations of the new.

A Summons from the Quantum Self

In the preparation stage the ego modality dominates. When we set ourselves to solve a problem we may begin by making a survey of what is known about the problem; we read and we imagine. We may break up the problem into parts to get a grasp on its solvability. But this is all preliminary. The real work begins when we start questioning what we have learned, including the problem itself. This is where we give imagination a chance.

The ego is skilled at gathering and digesting information, much like the central processing unit of a computer; it is in the quantum modality that we deal with the new, which the ego experiences as intuitive thought. Preparation always involves an initial intuition, a vague feeling of something new to be done. Imagination makes us sensitive to intuition. It all starts with asking the right question. Consider the following excerpt from *Alice in Wonderland:*

"It's always six o'clock now," the Hatter said mournfully.

A bright idea came into Alice's head. "Is that the reason so many tea-things are put out here?" she asked.

"Yes, that's it," said the Hatter with a sigh: "it's always tea-time, and we have no time to wash the things between whiles."

"Then you keep moving around, I suppose?" said Alice.

"Exactly so," said the Hatter: "as the things get used up."

"But what happens when you come to the beginning again?" Alice ventured to ask.

Alice asked the right question, intuiting that the context of the Mad Hatter's perpetual tea party was limited and change was needed. But in Wonderland her question was not followed up. The March Hare changed the subject. This is another thing about being creative: you must follow up when intuition exposes the limits of the present context. Think of intuition as a summons from the quantum self at the prodding of the archetypes.

One day artist Georgia O'Keeffe had an emotional crisis. She locked the door of her studio and faced the truth. She had been painting using other people's ideas! Was there nothing original that she could paint? At that moment she became open to the universe, and her quantum self gave her intuitive glimpses of abstract shapes, original images that had never before been collected in any problem space, human or machine. A moment of crisis brought her a sudden intuition of where she had to go.

One of Rabindranath Tagore's plays about creativity begins with the hero singing a song about the call of intuition (from the quantum self)—a very appropriate introduction to the preparation stage of the creative journey. When we don't hear this siren song, when we're content with ego stasis, creativity remains quiescent. The poet Robert Browning wrote only one poem during the first three years of his marriage to Elizabeth Barrett. He was too content!

The tangled interaction of intuition and preparation eventually leads to a destructuring of the old to make room for the new. We need a strong ego to handle this breakdown. In a way it's similar to entering the world of a surrealistic painting, where everything is distorted relative to the comfortable familiarity of our established belief system.

Creativity researcher Frank Barron has noted an apparent paradox in highly creative people; in test after test these people score high both on traits of ego-strength, such as coping with setbacks, and on the presence of ego-weakness, including neurosis and anxiety. The ego-weakness we see in creative people reflects the destructuring of their conceptual world, and their strength allows them to push through it into the new.

How do you know when you are properly prepared? The preparation stage must ultimately end up creating an open mind. During this stage the conviction grows that existing ideas, programs, and contexts are just not enough. We have to put to rest what we have accumulated in our search, and acknowledge, "I don't know." In the words of T. S. Eliot, "In order to arrive at what you do not know you must go by a way which is the way of ignorance." We learn to reside in this don't-know mind, this "cloud of unknowing," as a 12th-century Christian mystic described it; now we're in the second stage of the creative process, waiting for quantum consciousness to choose the new and the quantum self to communicate it to the ego.

What happens when our mind is open? When we prepare, we familiarize ourselves with what is possible, we search for footprints of great people's work. With an open mind our consciousness can access all the unconditioned states of the supramental and mental worlds. Indeed, consciousness is like a hologram: each little piece, every individual, has the information of the whole in his or her unconscious.

Even with the information superhighway at our disposal, our egos are privy only to fragments of what is available. Being open to the new and relegating the unconscious to quantum consciousness gives us access to all the supramental archetypes, and all as yet unexplored mental meaning. Leonardo da Vinci knew this when he wrote, "This is the real miracle, that all shapes, all colors, all images of every part of the universe are concentrated in a single point."

One other crucial aspect of preparedness is the pursuit of a burning question. Have you ever been driven by such a question? Without burning questions it's difficult to maintain the momentum required for insight. Everyone understands that stepping into a full bathtub causes the water to overflow. Only an Archimedes, faithful to his burning question, could see in that moment the answer for which he had been searching.

Mathematician G. Spencer-Brown puts it this way: "To arrive at the simplest truth, as Newton knew and practiced, requires years of contemplation. Not activity. Not reasoning. Not calculating. Not busy behavior of any kind. Not reading. Not talking. Simply bearing in mind what it is one needs to know."

An open mind and a burning question set the stage for the next phase of creativity—alternate work and relaxation, what I call "do-be-do-be-do." Work is more preparation, which makes sense; but what's the relaxation for? The relaxation is needed to incubate the egg of insight in the unconscious processing of new unlearned stimuli, conflicts, and ambiguities.[4]

Non-doing

Mullah Nasruddin was looking for something under a streetlight. A passerby began to help him look. But after a while, when he didn't find anything, he asked Nasruddin, "Mullah, what have you lost? What is it that we are looking for?"

"My key, I lost my key."

"But where did you lose it?"

"In my house," the mullah answered.

"Then why are you looking here?" shouted the helper in disbelief.

"There is more light here," said the mullah calmly.

Mechanical problem solvers look where the light is. They work hard to engage conscious processing, mostly reasoning. But if the problem requires a new context, or a new meaning from the transcendent domain of possibilities, the existing light doesn't help. The key is in the house, in the dark caverns of the unconscious. That's where we have to go, but how? By relaxing; by non-doing.

There are many examples of great creative people stopping their work, even during times of great success. Rabindranath Tagore took leave from his poetry, which he felt was becoming somewhat frivolous. He hibernated, with occasional forays into the spiritual literature of India. When he came back to work again he wrote *Gitanjali,* for which he received the Nobel Prize. Similarly, after American poet T. S. Eliot created the Nobel-winning *The Waste Land,* he, too, went into hibernation. When he returned he gave the world *Four Quartets,* poetry rich in spiritual insight and inspiration. Music virtuoso Yehudi Menuhin stopped playing the violin at age 40, and didn't pick it up again for 12 years. He needed a long stretch in which to rejuvenate his unconscious processing and inner creativity. Alternatively, many creative people engage in what Howard Gruber calls a network of enterprises, which enables them to unconsciously process one problem while consciously working on another.

How to Amplify Unconscious Processing

Most of us consciously react to associations; while reading a book, we get ideas and may write them down for later reference. But such conscious associations make only fragmentary contributions to a truly creative breakthrough. If we augment these associations with unbridled imagination and the analogies that association often ushers in, we do better. Imagination injects the process with new possibilities for unconscious processing; these possibilities interact with old possibilities producing more new possibilities, increasing the chances for the needed gestalt for creative insight.

Arthur Koestler noted that a different kind of association—an association of opposites that he called bisociation—may be more helpful to the creative process. "The basic bisociative pattern of the creative synthesis [is due to] the sudden interlocking of two previously unrelated skills, or matrices of thought," he declared. The more startling the bisociation, the more striking and novel is the creativity of the act.

A similar idea comes from psychologist Albert Rothenberg—he calls it Janusian thinking (after Janus, the Roman god with two faces). Rothenberg thinks that the idea for the Eugene O'Neill play *The Iceman Cometh* may have been the result of Janusian thinking, in the form of a joke: A household refrigerator needed attention. When the husband came home, he called up to his wife, "Has the iceman come yet?" The wife called down, "No, but he's breathing hard." Sex, Rothenberg notes, is a signifier of life, the opposite being the iceman, or death.

In the same vein, the philosopher Hegel emphasized the importance of dialectic thinking, using thesis and antitheses in order to reach synthesis. Are Koestler, Rothenberg, and Hegel right in saying that we are creative when we invite conflicts in the form of bisociations, Janusian thinking, and thesis-antithesis dialectics? They have to be, because it's impossible to really resolve those dichotomies using conscious analysis from known contexts. When confronted with such possibilities, we're trying to digest information that only quantum consciousness can process, and the new is invited in.

Charles Darwin made extensive use of metaphor in developing his theory of evolution. What is a metaphor? Grammatically, a metaphor compares two objects or things without the use of "as" or "like." (Classic examples include "All the world's a stage," and "A mighty fortress is our God.") A metaphor involves borrowing the attributes of one object (say, the stage), and ascribing them to another object (the world) in order to facilitate our understanding of that second object. From the quantum perspective, a metaphor helps trigger the development of a thought in a superposition involving the unknown. This is also an example of how ambiguous stimuli are crucial for unconscious processing. Any doubt about the old—is this right or is this wrong?—can give rise to ambiguity, which is why paradox and anomaly also play such important roles in creative insight.

Work and Relaxation, Striving and Surrender

Emily Dickinson called the intensity of the burning question "white heat." To maintain this intensity would not be humanly possible. Instead, the practical strategy is do-be-do-be-do: We alternate the intensity of the burning question with conscious relaxation. Why so much intensity? Intensity is needed because the mind's superpositions of possibilities generated in our unconscious processing tend to be dominated by our learned contexts. That intensity makes up for low probability of the new. Intense persistence, even in the face of repeated failures, is important because the more you collapse the mind's quantum state relative to the same question, the more you increase the chances of a new response. So in between bouts of effort, sit quietly, allowing the waves of possibility to spread, forming bigger and bigger pools of possibility for quantum consciousness to choose from.

A woman goes to a fabric store and orders 50 yards of material for her wedding dress. When the shopkeeper expresses surprise, saying, "Madam, you only need a few yards," the woman replies, "My fiancé is a doer who would rather search than find."

The creative knows the importance of being, the importance of do-be-do-be-do. The creative does not get stuck in the joys of searching, but knows how to find.

Marie Curie did her doctoral thesis on the emission of electromagnetic radiation from uranium, but she got bogged down in finding the reason for the radiation. Her husband, Pierre, joined her research, and their joint perseverance eventually produced the insight that a new element, radium, was responsible. Clearly, the creative individual's ego has to be both strong and highly motivated to be persistent and to handle the anxiety that the quantum jump into new insight creates. The contribution of the ego is justly recognized in the inventor Thomas Edison's saying that genius is 2 percent inspiration and 98 percent perspiration.

Bertrand Russell wrote about his use of alternate work and relaxation, of striving and unconscious processing in his creative work, as follows:

It appeared that first contemplating a book on some subject, and after giving serious preliminary attention to it, I needed a period of subconscious incubation which could not be hurried and was if anything impeded by deliberate thinking. Sometimes, I would find after a time, that I had made a mistake, and that I could not write the book I had had in mind. But often I was more fortunate. Having, by a time of very intense concentration, planted the problem in my subconscious, it would germinate underground until, suddenly, the solution emerged with blinding clarity, so that it only remained to write down what had appeared as if in a revelation.[5]

Werner Heisenberg had a rule for his doctoral students. After initially discussing their Ph.D. problem with them, he told his students not to work on it for two weeks, but just to relax. He appreciated the value of alternating doing with being. Rabindranath Tagore, who also understood this alternate play of will and surrender, described it in one of his songs. Since no translation from the Bengali is available, I will paraphrase:

> When infinity calls
> I want to fly to its Siren's song;
> I want to hold the infinity in my palm
> NOW.
> I forget I don't have wings,
> That I am too damn local.

This is the stage of striving that creative people know all too well. Tagore understood the stage of relaxation as well:

> On lazy afternoons, sunshine like butter,
> Swaying trees cast dancing shadows.
> I am bathed in the light of infinity.
> Unattended, still it fills my mind's sky.
> I process unaware, in silent bliss.

Tagore also knew that this bliss does not last long before inspiration fuels the desire for manifestation again:

> Oh infinity, oh great infinity—
> Go on, play your flute, sing your song.
> Let me forget
> That the doors of my room are closed.
> I am restless with creative energy.

Doing and being, will and surrender.

The Aha Insight

After a long play of alternating will and surrender, persistence and relaxation, conscious and unconscious processing, our quantum consciousness recognizes and chooses the gestalt, the pattern of the little pieces that together make up the new meaning and context, the breakthrough pattern. From the superpositions of possibilities that have accumulated during the creative journey, we collapse the gestalt and see it as separate from ourselves. The breakthrough, as I have discussed before, usually comes during the relaxation phase.

Einstein once asked a psychologist at Princeton, "Why is it I get my best ideas in the morning while I'm shaving?" The psychologist answered that consciousness needs to let go of its inner controls in order for new ideas to emerge. This is the point. In ordinary waking consciousness, the ego's inner controls override the preconscious primary experiences through which the quantum self communicates to the ego. When we're relaxing—shaving is a good example; dreaming, bathing, and daydreaming are others—the normally preconscious experience of the insight breaks through.

I vividly remember the day when I came to the realization that all things are made of consciousness, not matter, and that from this vantage point we have to develop a science within consciousness. For many years I had been researching the idea that consciousness collapses the quantum possibility wave, but I was struggling to explain how a consciousness with such power could emerge in the material brain. One day, on vacation, I was explaining the difficulty to a mystic friend, Joel Morwood. He did not agree with my view and, at some point in the middle of a big argument, made a statement long familiar to me: "There is nothing but God." Suddenly I knew that there is nothing but consciousness, that matter consists of possibilities of consciousness, and that it was possible to conduct scientific work on the basis of the primacy of consciousness.

I could already see glimpses of the new science; I already knew that it would resolve all the paradoxes of the old science and explain all the anomalous data, but I was in no hurry. I stayed in the glow of that aha moment for a long time. That insight was instrumental in the subsequent research and development of the paradigm of science within consciousness that culminated in *The Self-Aware Universe.*

Remember the time lag between primary and secondary experiences? Our preoccupation with the secondary processes distracts us from our quantum self, making it difficult to experience the quantum level of our operation. A creative experience is one of the few occasions when we directly experience the quantum modality with its inherent cosmic awareness, and it is this spontaneous encounter that produces *ananda* (Sanskrit for limitlessness)—the spiritual joy of the "aha" insight. This is what Rabindranath Tagore was writing about when he described his experience of the light that I see as the quantum self:

> Light, my light, the world-filling light;
> The eye-kissing light, heart-sweetening light.
> Ah the light dances, my darling,
> At the center of my life. The light strikes,
> My darling, the chords of my love;
> The sky opens, the wind runs wild,
> Laughter passes over the earth.[6]

Similar peak experiences of ananda also happen in inner creativity. In spiritual traditions these experiences are given exalted names such as samadhi, or satori, or being in the Holy Spirit.

The Encounter in Manifestation

The fourth and final stage of creativity, the manifestation stage, is the encounter of idea and form. The self in its ego modality has to develop a form for the creative idea generated in stage three. After doing so it must sort out and organize its elements, and verify that it works. The importance of form is seen in studies done with children's drawings, which show that until children learn certain forms, they are unable to express certain creative ideas.

Even Einstein had trouble making the transition from idea to form. Many times he complained about his struggle to find the right form, the right mathematics, to express his idea of a unified theory of all the forces of the world, the problem that engaged him in the latter part of his life. The fact is that even after the brain has made a preliminary map of a novel mental idea, the unavailability of form in the ego's known repertoire may send you hunting for ideas once again.

For many acts of creation, finding form in the outer world is just a difficult business, literally. An architect's vision may never find expression in the outer world because of economics. Michelangelo's struggle with creative manifestation included the struggle for more marble. Even after their insight about the existence of a new chemical element, radium, it took Marie Curie and her husband Pierre four years and processing of tons of uranium to isolate radium.

When Nikos Kazantzakis first attempted to write *Zorba the Greek,* he expressed his frustration with form in this way:

> I wrote, I crossed out. I could not find suitable words. Sometimes they were dull and soulless, sometimes indecently gaudy, at other times abstract and full of air, lacking a warm body. I knew what I planned to say when I set out, but the shiftless, unbridled words dragged me elsewhere. . . . Realizing the time had not arrived, that the secret metamorphosis inside the seed still had not been completed, I stopped.[7]

The creative struggle between ego and quantum consciousness can bring agony, no doubt. But it's well worth it, not only because of quantum leaps of insight but because the struggle eventually gives way to the play of form and idea (figure 20). The result is what we experience as flow. Then the pen writes itself, the dancer becomes the dance, and the golfer finds himself in the zone. Many creative people talk about the experience of flow. "It is like diving into the pond—then you start to swim," said the novelist D. H. Lawrence. "Once the instinct and intuition get into the brush tip, the picture happens, if it is to be a picture at all."

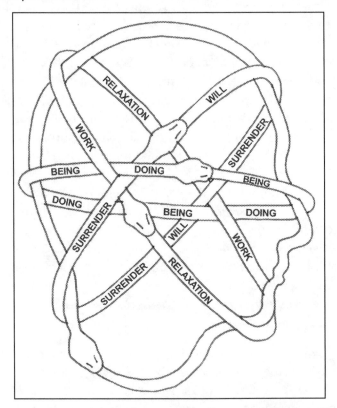

Figure 20: The tangled hierarchies of the various stages
of the creative process (after Charles Hampden-Turner).

Novelist Gertrude Stein, in conversation with the author John Preston, said the same thing. "Think of the writing in terms of discovery, which is to say that creation must take place between the pen and the paper, not before in a thought or afterwards in a recasting."

Can We Live in the Zone? The Story of Kalidasa

In ancient India there was a famous king named Vikrama. He had two poets in his court, but he favored one, Kalidasa, over the other. Many members of the court could see no difference in quality between the poetry of the two poets—a poem is a poem is a poem. So one day they put their question to the king. Why do you favor Kalidasa over the other court poet, when to us they both seem to write poetry equally well? The king decided that it was time for a demonstration.

The court assembled in the king's garden in the dormancy of early springtime. Many trees were leafless, but one tree looked dead. The secondary poet was summoned first. Pointing to the dead tree, the king said to him, "Please compose a verse based on what you see." The poet complied, and his verse can be translated as follows: "There is dead wood ahead." When Kalidasa was given the same task, he came up with, "A great tree, void of juice, shines ahead."

The courtiers never again complained. Whereas the lesser poet saw the verse-making as a problem and solved it adequately, Kalidasa jumped contexts. He was able to see shining from the leafless tree because he himself was alive and spontaneous; he was in flow. Whereas the other poet was acting from his ego when he composed his poem, Kalidasa was acting from an encounter with the quantum self, so his poem created itself.

Many poets live in the zone. Walt Whitman wrote:

> To me, every hour of the light and dark is a miracle,
> Every inch of space is a miracle,
> Every square yard of the surface of the earth
> is spread with the same,
> Every cubic foot of the interior swarms with the same.[8]

I believe every one of us has this ability, this creative potential. We just have to manifest it.

Melody seeks to fetter herself in rhythm.
While the rhythm flows back to melody.
Idea seeks the body in form,
Form its freedom in the idea.
The infinite seeks the touch of the finite,
The finite its release in the infinite.
What drama is this between creation and destruction—
This ceaseless to-and-fro between idea and form?
Bondage is striving after freedom,
And freedom seeking rest in bondage.[9]
—Tagore

PART III

CAN ANYONE BE CREATIVE?

CHAPTER 10

Is Creative Motivation a Drive from the Unconscious?

Am I right in my conviction that anyone can be creative? Or is creativity only for those few people with unusual motivation or talent, or both? In this chapter, we'll take a closer look at the question of motivation.

Sigmund Freud, who pioneered the idea of the unconscious, saw it as the repository for repressed instincts, mostly related to sexuality. According to Freud, libido finds expression in creativity for well-adapted people and in neurosis for the maladapted. Freud saw creative people as having an unusual capacity to sublimate the sexual drive and to process its unconscious images into socially acceptable forms that could appear novel and creative. For example, Leonardo da Vinci's particular style of portraying women like Mona Lisa originates, according to Freud, in the repressed Oedipal feelings of what his mother's smile meant to da Vinci.

Freud saw creativity as a close cousin of neurosis: The unconscious drive that motivates a creative solution may motivate a neurotic solution as well.[1]

An artist is once more in rudiments an introvert, not far removed from neurosis. He is oppressed by excessively powerful instinctual needs. He desires to win honor, power, wealth, fame, and the love of women; but he lacks the means for achieving these satisfactions.

Consequently, like any other unsatisfied man, he turns away from reality and transfers all his interest and his libido, too, to the wishful construction of his life of fantasy, whence the path might lead to neurosis.

Freud also saw a connection between the imagination of children and adult creativity, insisting that the "freely rising" fantasies and ideas of adult creativity are nothing but a continuation of childhood play and daydreaming. The power of the creative person lies in accepting these daydreams and putting them to good use, whereas the neurotic suppresses them. For Freud, a person arrives at "achievements of special perfection" when his unconscious processes adapt to normal ego functioning.

The quantum theory of consciousness supports Freud's basic idea of what is now called the personal unconscious. If we are conditioned to avoid certain emotional memories—perhaps because of childhood trauma—the probability becomes overwhelming that possibilities corresponding to these memories are never collapsed from superpositions of quantum possibilities that we process in our unconscious. Such repressed possibilities, however, may influence the collapse of subsequent states, and thus seem creative or neurotic depending on the degree of the subject's adaptation.

But Freud's theory that creative people just convert unconscious socially unacceptable neurotic images to socially acceptable novel creative products is at best only part of the story. When van Gogh paints *The Starry Night* as a swirling mass of cosmic energy, the quantum possibilities of meaning for his unconscious processing consist not only of the contributions of his repression (neurotic or not), but also of his capacity to transcend his personality. The first gives his painting form, whereas the second gives it the formless, universal emotion that connects directly to the viewer.

Transforming Poison into Nectar

Russian film director Sergei Eisenstein was compelled to depict cruelty in his films. Sergei grew up as an abused child, so cruelty was no stranger to him, and such a painful childhood must have produced a lot of repression. Is his depiction of cruelty in films another example of Freudian creativity then? Not quite, because his films often end in transformative, uplifting, positive emotions. What caused the change?

During childhood Eisenstein watched a French movie that influenced his vision and moved him into a new direction. In the film, a sergeant in the army who had become a prisoner forced to work on a farm was branded on the shoulder as punishment for making love to the farmer's wife. A strange transformation took place in the way Eisenstein looked at cruelty: He was no longer sure who was being cruel to whom.

> In my childhood it [the film] gave me nightmares. . . . Sometimes I became the sergeant, sometimes the branding iron. I would grab hold of his shoulder. Sometimes it seemed to be my own shoulder. At other times it was someone else's. I no longer knew who was branding whom.[2]

This is the thing—in the quantum modality evil is not something separate from us. When we realize this intuitively, then evil can be transformed. The integrative insight that took place in Eisenstein's own psyche eventually enabled him to use the ugliness of cruelty to achieve great beauty in his films. If you've ever watched *Battleship Potemkin* you know what I mean. English professor and author John Briggs has given a name to this ability to transform the poison of negative emotions into the nectar of the positive: "omnivalence."[3] In another time the poet John Keats called it "negative capability."

Shakespeare knew about this transformative aspect of creativity when he wrote *The Tempest*. Creativity can metamorphose the horrible stuff of a cadaver into "something rich and strange," he wrote. But our rational ego must yield to the alchemy of our quantum mode.

> Full fathom five thy father lies
> Of his bones are coral made;
> Those are pearls that were his eyes;
> Nothing of him that doth fade
> But doth suffer a sea change
> Into something rich and strange;

Sea nymphs hourly ring his knell;
Hark, I hear them; Ding-Dong Bell.

The impact of such a transformative journey is enormous, as it serves the evolutionary movement of consciousness that opens all humanity to the energies of love.

Motivation from the Collective Unconscious

Carl Jung recognized that the sublimation of libido is only a partial criterion for creativity, not a sufficient one. Jung viewed the unconscious not only as personal, but also as collective—a repository of collectively suppressed memory available for all humanity, that transcends the boundaries of time, space, and culture. In this way Jung identified additional motivation for creativity in the drive from the collective unconscious. He found that creative ideas often emerge in the garb of universal symbols (such as the hero) that have become known as Jungian archetypes.[4] Said Jung: "The creative process, so far as we are able to follow it at all, consists in the unconscious activation of an archetypal image, and in elaborating and shaping this image into the finished work."

Thus for Jung, creativity is a result of an unconscious drive, yes, but not only one from the personal, repressed unconscious of Freudian vintage but also one that evokes archetypal images from the collective unconscious.

Consider the chemist Friedrich August Kekule's discovery of the structure of the benzene molecule. At that time all known bonding occurred in open, linear arrangements. Within this context the solution to the benzene problem eluded everyone. Kekule's famous breakthrough came to him during a reverie state in which he saw a snake biting its own tail, and realized the bonding in this case must be circular. According to Jung, the dream image that triggered Kekule's insight is a prime example of an archetypal image from the collective unconscious—in this case the uroboros symbol.

Curiosity comes from the drive to make manifest what is previously unconscious and unmanifest. Initially our curiosity is mild and restricted to areas of conflict. The archetypes are calling us, but we are not hearing their sound as more than a whisper. Realizing that we have an obstruction, we clean it up by making the conflict conscious: creativity, Freudian style. Next we begin to discover transformation. We have dreams involving Jungian archetypes, and become more curious and more motivated to explore them: creativity, Jung style.

The totality of consciousness seeks to know itself through this purposeful drive of the unconscious, so its movements are often intricate, even bizarre—so much so that we can see them as mere coincidences or chance events. Close scrutiny reveals otherwise. Carl Jung called seemingly meaningful coincidences—one in the outer arena and one in the inner arena of experience—"synchronicities," and he saw an important role for synchronicity in creativity.[5] Jung speculated that these coincidences had a common cause, which we now know to be downward causation. The qualities of this cause, and its criteria for creative expression, are elaborated in the next chapter.

Care to take a fantasy tour?
See yourself approaching a forest dense and dark.
What's down there? An underground house,
Dark and mysterious, evoking childish
Memories of witches scary.
What is your tendency?
Take risk, go down, explore?
Or stay in the filtered light of safety?

CHAPTER 11

Attuning to the Creative Universe and Its Purpose

All creative acts, fundamental or situational, inner or outer, share one feature: They are goal-directed. Creative acts take place not as the result of random forays, but when somebody does something purposeful to context or meaning that adds new value based on some sort of a future vision in mind, however vague.

Two kinds of purpose guide human acts. The first kind, the more common, relates to what we can call relative purpose—it has a social origin and is relative to space, time, and culture. Industry, technology, government, and individual artists all serve some relative purpose. Solving problems that society faces and inventing things to satisfy a particular desire in society serve a relative purpose, too.

The second kind of purposefulness recognizes that the aim of creative acts is itself fluid. There is a general pattern of purpose and design in creative acts, but the final goal is not fixed. It is opportunistic and contingent upon the situation. The theater director Peter Brook expresses this idea perfectly:

> What is necessary is an incomplete design; a design that has clarity without rigidity; one that can be called "open" as against "shut." . . . A true theater designer will think of his

designs as being all the time in motion, in action, in relation to what the actor brings to the scene as it unfolds. The later he makes his decision, the better.[1]

Chance in Creativity, or Is It Synchronicity?

Alexander Fleming's discovery of penicillin is an interesting case of creativity involving supposedly chance events. According to Fleming's biographer, Gwyn MacFarlane, while Fleming was on vacation, a mycologist on the floor below Fleming's lab happened to isolate a strong strain of the penicillin mold, which somehow found its way to a petri dish in Fleming's lab. Unusually cold weather for that time of the year helped the mold spores to grow and simultaneously prevented the growth of bacteria. Then the temperature rose, and bacteria grew everywhere except in the petri dish. This attracted Fleming's attention: What was in the petri dish that prevented bacteria from growing? This is a case in which "an incredible string of chance events" gave rise to momentous creativity. But was this really just chance? I would call this an act of synchronicity, and I think Jung would agree.

Regardless of what you call it, if chance can work its miracles by accidental coincidences, then why not use chance deliberately? Musician John Cage experimented with the role of chance in musical creativity. Even improvised music like jazz or East Indian music follows known patterns. Cage felt that to discover truly new music in the 20th century, he had to give chance a chance. So he began to mix in synthesized music and all sorts of natural and artificial sounds to create his own unique sound. At one of his concerts, no musical instrument or voice greeted the listeners, but only the random noise of somebody's sneeze or people's restless movements!

In the realm of art, Robert Rauschenberg performed a similar experiment. In his youth Rauschenberg became disillusioned with expressionist painting. Instead, Rauschenberg felt that the paint itself should be treated as an object, and then the idea came to him: Why not use objects? So he created some interesting paintings of

New York City by pasting little bits and pieces of real New York on a canvas.

I think it is fair to say that neither Cage nor Rauschenberg's ideas got much long-term traction, although they certainly have their place in the history of modern art. How about Jackson Pollock? He created some great paintings by pouring paint over a canvas in a seemingly random way, much like writing a poem with arbitrary combinations of words. This is why many cheats—artists and art dealers included—try to make large sums of money selling fake Pollocks. But when University of Oregon physicist Richard Taylor was asked by the Pollock-Krasner Foundation to investigate such fraud, he discovered that Pollock's paintings are not random at all. Instead they depict fractal patterns found in nature. These patterns are soothing to the human eye, which explains the artist's popular appeal.

The comic-strip character Dilbert says, "If creativity were anything but random, someone would have figured out the algorithm by now." Many scientific materialists continue to think this way. But if deliberate use of chance fails to produce a creative product, why hold on to the idea that accidental chance has anything to do with creativity? Instead, let's see the latter as synchronistic events—events chosen by nonlocal consciousness that give the appearance of blind chance or mere coincidence.

Earlier in this book, I discussed Calder's development of the mobile sculpture, where a seemingly chance coincidence played a momentous role in Calder's work. By meeting abstract artist Piet Mondrian and seeing his work, Calder suddenly saw the value of abstract sculpture. Was it pure chance that Mondrian visited Calder? Jung would say it was synchronicity, and I would have to agree. Anyone engaged in creative work can find many such seeming coincidences—opening the right page of a book, looking at a picture at the right moment, hearing something at the right time, etc. Nobel laureate Murray Gell-Mann was giving a physics lecture on some strange elementary particles when he committed a slip of the tongue only to realize in a flash of insight that the idea conveyed by the slip was the answer to the problem he was working on. (A Jungian slip, perhaps?)

In 1993 I was on my first radio show when an old lady asked me, "What happens when we die?" I didn't know! The question took me aback, but I recovered, and did nothing more about it. A month or so later, an elderly Theosophist expressed interest in learning more about my just-published book *The Self-Aware Universe,* but in truth he started to fill *my* head with Theosophical ideas, such as reincarnation. At first, I did not take them seriously. Then, as I was dreaming one night I heard a voice speaking to me, but I couldn't make out its meaning. The voice grew louder and louder until I could clearly hear, "*The Tibetan Book of the Dead* is correct, and it's your job to prove it." The admonition was so loud it woke me up. I started taking reincarnation seriously after that.

A couple of months later a graduate student whose boyfriend had died came to my office for help with her grieving. I told her that I was no therapist, but she insisted on making regular visits. Then one day, I was trying to console her with the idea that maybe her boyfriend's subtle body, or energetic body, survived his death—an idea I had picked up during my Hindu upbringing but had never taken seriously. Suddenly a thought came to me: Suppose the essence of the subtle body and the vital body we live in every day consists of quantum possibilities, and that consciousness mediates between them (and also the physical realm) nonlocally? Could that not solve the problem of dualism as well as that of survival of the soul from one lifetime to the next? Subsequently, I wrote the book *Physics of the Soul.*

Some time later I was teaching a graduate course connecting quantum physics and Jungian psychology to a class of depth psychology students, but I was getting nowhere. One day I gave a talk on the idea that the physical, vital, mental, and supramental aspects of the self are all quantum possibilities of consciousness. Even this huge new idea, a solution to the mind-matter dualism problem, elicited no excitement in my students. In desperation I told them about how I had made this discovery: the story above. When I finished, the class was buzzing with excitement. From then on I had no problem of credibility with my students.

Meditation teacher and author Jack Kornfield provides us with a wonderful example of synchronicity in inner creativity. At a meditation retreat led by Kornfield, a woman was struggling with emotions arising from childhood abuse. At this retreat she finally found forgiveness in her heart for the man who had abused her. When she came home from the retreat, she found a letter in her mailbox from the man, with whom she had had no contact for 15 years. In the letter the man asked for her forgiveness. When was the letter written? The very same day the woman had completed her own act of forgiveness.

There is no doubt about it: Our interconnected roots in consciousness (figure 21) nourish creativity. Like Kornfield's forgiving woman, when we are involved in a creative insight, we become aligned with the movement of the whole, with nonlocal consciousness. That movement has no local boundary; it neither originates nor ends in one particular brain-mind complex.

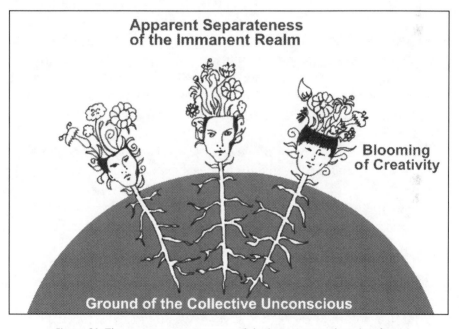

Figure 21: The apparent separateness of the immanent realm arises from the unity of the collective consciousness. Our creativity is nourished by our interconnected roots via quantum consciousness.

Creative Evolution of the Cosmos and Tuning
In to the Cosmic Purpose

The archetypal themes of consciousness remain potential until matter with which to manifest them evolves to sufficient complexity, and self-referential life originates. When the human form emerges, biological functions manifest, and are represented as organs at the various chakras. Then one day the meaning-giving mind evolves in the form of the neocortex, and on that day consciousness takes a giant leap—the ability to conceive of itself as separate from the world, to be aware of that distinction.

The details that anthropologists study and codify show that the way our mind processes meaning has evolved dramatically since our primitive days as hunters and gatherers. Back then we were most interested in giving meaning to the physical in order to survive. Then we went through a stage when we gave meaning to our feelings, to the energies of vital movement; we developed a vital mind. This took place during the time humans were developing small-scale agriculture using implements like the hoe. No doubt men and women working together in the fields facilitated the development of the vital mind.

With the development of the plough and large-scale agriculture, and the leisure time it created for the wealthy, we became interested in the meaning of mental processing itself; thus began the age of the rational mind that we are still exploring. It's becoming clear that in the next stage the mind will give meaning to intuition, leading to an intuitive mind. Outliers among us have been exploring the intuitive mind for millennia, but this ability has not percolated through to society as a whole. When we're all attuned to processing the meaning of what we intuit, and to living the discovered meaning, then we will bring heaven to this earth. That's where we are going in our creative evolution.[2]

We become most creative in our lives when we recognize that the cosmos is trying to act through us, and we become aligned with that cosmic purpose. As novelist Nikos Kazantzakis put it, one has to open up a personal riverbed through which the universe may flow. Is this even possible? Rabindranath Tagore describes an experience as a boy that exemplifies this point:

> I still remember the day in my childhood when I was made to struggle across my lessons in a first primer . . . Suddenly, I came to a rhymed sentence of combined words, which may be translated thus—"It rains, the leaves tremble." At once I came to a world wherein I recovered my full meaning. My mind touched the creative realm of expression, and at that moment I was no longer a mere student with his mind muffled by spelling lessons, enclosed by classroom. The rhythmic picture of tremulous leaves beaten by the rain opened before my mind the world which does not merely carry information, but a harmony with my being. The unmeaning fragments lost their individual isolation and my mind reveled in the unity of a vision. In a similar manner, on that morning in the village, the facts of my life suddenly appeared to me in a luminous unity of truth. . . . I felt sure that some Being who comprehended me and my world was seeking his best expression in all my experiences, uniting them into an ever-widening individuality which is a spiritual work of art.[3]

When Albert Einstein was five years old and ill in bed, his father brought him a magnetic compass. The fact that the needle pointed to the north regardless of how he turned the case gave young Einstein quite a thrill, and according to physicist Gerald Holton, also gave Einstein one of his themes of future research: continuity. I think it did much more: It gave young Einstein a sense of wonder about the nature of the universe that directed his scientific pursuits for the rest of his life. As he later said about his search, "[I have wanted to] experience the universe as a single significant whole."

Psychologist Howard Gruber discovered in Darwin's notebooks the recurrent image of a tree, an "image of wide scope" that seemed to have a profound influence on Darwin. The tree of life symbolized Darwin's feeling of oneness with the universal purpose of evolution; in it Darwin saw the grand scale of biological research: "The grand question which every naturalist ought to have before him when dissecting a whale, or classifying a mite, a fungus, or an infusorian is, What are the laws of Life?" This awareness led Darwin to his theory of evolution, incomplete as it was; Darwin failed to include purposiveness in his theory, as he had intended.

"It is the discovery of my relationship with the universe . . . that propels my translation," said poet and artist Carolyn Mary Kleefeld. At the age of seven Kleefeld saw dust particles dancing in the sunlight streaming through a window, which gave rise to her first creative expression, and it lead to a life devoted to creativity.

Novelist Henry James was at a dinner party when a woman made a comment about a fight over an estate between mother and son. Mundane conversation piece? Not for James, who was inspired to write *The Spoils of Poynton.* Experiences of subtle shades of meaning—of nuance—are often signs of synchronicity.

Virginia Woolf describes her first childhood experience of nuance with vivid imagery:

> If life has a base that it stands upon, if it is a bowl that one fills and fills and fills—then my bowl without a doubt stands upon this memory. It is of lying half asleep, half awake, in bed in the nursery at St. Ives. It is of hearing the waves breaking, one, two, one two, behind the yellow blind. It is of hearing the blind draw its little acorn across the floor as the wind blew the blind out. It is of lying and hearing this splash and seeing this light, and feeling, it is almost impossible that I should be here; of feeling the purest ecstasy I can conceive.[4]

Woolf's early experience spread its gentle influence to the greatest of her novels, *To the Lighthouse* and *The Waves.*

What happens in these experiences of synchronicity? They are events of primary awareness—a momentary encounter with the quantum self, a glimpse of quantum nonlocality. Such an encounter leads to a wider vision, producing images of expanded scope. It might also include the ecstasy of a peak experience, inspiring a personal sense of purpose that is in tune with the purpose of the universe.

When you were a child you had such moments many times, but you may not remember them. Not knowing the importance of that kind of sensitivity to the world, you kept your insight to yourself until it was relegated to the dustbin of memory.

John Briggs believes that early development of the sensitivity of nuance is crucial for later creativity. Maybe so. But can you redevelop that creative sensitivity now, as an adult? I think you can. You are potentially the quantum self but you misidentify solely with the ego! To be sensitive to the world, you must give sway to your quantum self again, as you did when you were a child; this re-enchantment is the goal of inner creativity. There are many examples of late starters in creativity. Personalizing the purpose of the universe is an important key, and it can be done at any age.

Once you personalize universal purpose, the creative spirit of the archetypes of quantum consciousness manifests in the quantum self's attempt to guide you. You resonate with these lines from William Wordsworth, who felt that he was given the gift "to see into the life of things."

> The mind of man is fashioned and built up
> Even as a strain of music, I believe
> That there are spirits which, when they would form
> A favored being, from his very dawn
> Of infancy do open out the clouds
> As at the touch of lightning, seeking him
> With gentle visitation—quiet powers,
> Retired, and seldom recognized, yet kind,
> And to the very meanest not unknown—
> With me, though rarely, in my boyish days
> They communed.[5]
> —Wordsworth

CHAPTER 12

Where Do Creative Traits Come From?

In some empirical studies, creative people as a group are found to be imaginative, self-confident, original, to be risk takers, divergent as well as convergent thinkers, and hard workers. Trait theorists maintain that these capacities, among others, separate highly creative people from the rest of us.

Two boys in France were given the task of taking a short trip and then coming back and reporting on it. When they came back, the first boy was asked, "So, what did you see?" The boy shrugged his shoulders. "Nothing much." Sound familiar? But the second boy, in answer to the same question, said with luminous eyes, "I have seen *so* much." Then he proceeded to describe it all in glowing detail. The first boy was a typical child; after some patient prompting he could have come up with some interesting anecdotes. The second boy grew up to be renowned novelist Victor Hugo.

A trait theorist would say that Victor Hugo was a genius because he had the special trait of divergent thinking. Most trait theorists think that the qualities connected with creativity are measurable, so they have developed tests to quantify those traits to ascertain people's creative potential. These creativity tests are reminiscent of IQ tests for intelligence, but are much more elaborate and cover many dimensions of personality, including emotions and values (whereas IQ tests tend to concentrate on rational thinking alone).

Divergent and Convergent Thinking

Widely used tests by creativity researchers E. P. Torrance and J. P. Guilford emphasize how we learn and think, and whether we have a tendency to think about a problem in many ways or to focus quickly on one particular way—that is, whether one's cognitive style is *divergent* or *convergent*.[1] Suppose you ask a child to name two days of the week that begin with the letter *t*; at first he says, "Tuesday and Thursday," but on second thought he adds, "also today and tomorrow." At once you know you're looking at a divergent thinker.

Edward de Bono, the Maltese physician, inventor, and author, gives an excellent example of divergent thinking (which de Bono calls lateral thinking).[2] In this example a moneylender approaches a man deeply in debt as he and his daughter are out for a stroll on a pebble-strewn path. "Here are two pebbles," says the moneylender, dropping them into a bag, "a white one and a dark one. If your daughter, without looking, can pick the white one from the bag, your debt will be excused. But if she picks the black one, then she is mine."

Using convergent thinking one would expect a 50-50 chance of choosing the white pebble, so the borrower agreed to the moneylender's game of chance. But his daughter, thinking divergently (and also probably listening to her intuition), knew better than to trust the lender. She suspected that both pebbles might be dark. What to do? She put her hand in the bag and took out a pebble, but stumbled awkwardly, dropping it on the pebble-strewn path before its color could be seen. She then exclaimed, "How clumsy of me. I've lost it! But, happily, we can tell the color of the pebble I drew by looking at the one remaining in the bag. Ah, it's black. So the one I drew must have been white."

On the face of it, how can we doubt the relevance of divergent thinking to creativity? How can you discover the new without a mind open to considering many possibilities before homing in on one? But there is more subtlety here. In a survey, when creative scientists were asked if they use much divergent thinking, they said, no, they use convergent thinking, narrowing down the possible answers.

Are Torrance, Guilford, and company wrong, then? Not necessarily. Creative people do engage in divergent thinking, even though they mostly do so in the unconscious mind, in the realm of possibility. They allow unresolved ambiguity to proliferate possibilities via unconscious processing. Then, when the time is ripe, creative ideas emerge in a flash of insight that may seem to them to be the outcome of a logical process of convergent thinking.

Do Traits Come from Genes and Brains?

Scientific materialists believe in local causes for every effect, and creativity is no exception. Since for them, only elementary particles have causal power, the causal chain for creativity must be something like this: Elementary particles make atoms, atoms make molecules, some of them are DNA, portions of which are genes. Genes make traits that motivate people to be creative because creativity has survival value. Genes also are responsible for all the rest of the behavioral habits we need to bring our creativity to fruition.

Francis Galton, an eminent scientist of the 19th century, published a book in 1869, *Hereditary Genius,* in which he attempted to show "that a man's natural abilities are derived by inheritance, under exactly the same limitations as are the form and the physical features of the whole organic world." Indeed, if you go through Galton's list of the genealogy of talented people (whether they are all geniuses can be debated), you will be impressed. One of the claims he made, for example, is that "at least 40% of the poets (number studied: 56) have had eminently gifted relations."

Galton made his list even before we knew how heredity works. The later discovery of genes was considered a great support for Galton's hypothesis of the inheritance of creativity traits. But gradually, with more understanding, the excitement subsided. No creativity genes were ever found. Nor do genes express themselves in any kind of one-to-one correspondence with the macroscopic traits of a person, especially personality traits. The making of biological forms, including the pathways of the brain, as we discussed earlier, results from complicated interactions between genetic inheritance, morphogenetic fields, and the environment. Additionally, the ego development of the person must play some role. It is very difficult to separate genetic from morphogenetic field and environmental influences, but one glaring fact in support of the latter is that it is extremely rare for the children of highly creative people to end up highly creative.

In the 1980s there was a lot of hoopla about creativity being a property of the brain's right hemisphere, which is holistic in its processing, as opposed to the left hemisphere, which is calculating, and reason-based. A prevailing theory at that time suggested that many people, conditioned by society to develop only the left brain, fail to become creative because they have not cultivated their right brains. But research has failed to identify any physical location, such as the right brain, as the wellspring for creative ideas.

Does Behavioral Conditioning Generate Traits and Motivation?

As I mentioned earlier, there are many surveys supporting claims that personality traits are essential to creativity, and that they can be learned. There are, however, surveys that negate these claims by trait theorists.

One of these surveys was carried out in the 1950s by Donald MacKinnon, who studied a group of 40 of the most creative architects in the United States.[3] He had two other control groups. One was chosen at random from a directory of architects—we'll call it the unrelated group. The second group was also unrelated, with one difference: each member of this group had worked with one of the members of the creative group mentioned above, for at least two years—we'll call this the associate group.

In a series of multidimensional tests, the creative architects differed from the unrelated group in many personality dimensions. They scored much higher on appreciation of aesthetics and much lower on the appreciation of economics. The creative group also scored much higher in sensitivity to feelings, and they were significantly less social.

This was the good news for trait theories. The bad news was that in 39 of 40 personality measures, the associate group performed similarly to the creative group. How can we say that personality traits are unique to creatives when, clearly, non-creatives also have them?

Does this mean that personality traits are not important here? No, the difference of traits between the creative and the unrelated non-creative group was too striking to ignore. But the associate group differed from the creative group in only one aspect, which proved to make a significant difference. The associates all lacked aesthetics—the quality that calls people to creative architecture.

Learned personality traits do not guarantee creative achievements. Compelling data for the efficacy of behavioral conditioning come from animal training, but animals have very weak egos, or little capacity to override conditioning. This is not the case for human beings. But if personality traits are not genetic and not learned, where *do* the traits of creative people come from?

Are Creative Traits a Legacy from Past Incarnations?

There is another possibility beside genes, brains, and environmental conditioning. The traits necessary for creativity could be a gift from past incarnations. But is reincarnation valid from a scientific perspective? I'll outline the supporting data in the next chapter, but for now I'd like to share my belief that the traits that we see in creative people are very special and require many lives to establish, which is why creative people seem to evoke them so easily whereas the rest of us rely on extraordinary effort.

This is a good place to reiterate the idea of morphogenetic fields that correlate with our organs. Creative work during one life modifies the brain, producing neural circuits that support creative behavior, which means the correlated morphogenetic fields must also change along with the brain. The propensities of these changes are nonlocal, therefore it makes sense that when we reincarnate we inherit these nonlocal learnings of the brain's morphogenetic field, which builds us a brain with highly developed pathways of creative behavior.

Dogma says, "Believe the data
That fit your model of the world
And ignore the rest."

The world says, "Ignore the dogma
And extend your model
To fit the world."

CHAPTER 13

Creativity and Reincarnation

Earlier I posited my belief that anyone can be highly creative, but the issue is nuanced. For one thing, in order for any endeavor to be successful, a high degree of motivation and strength of intention are required. How creative we are depends on how badly we want to find soul-satisfying answers to our inquiries: How strong is our need to know? Anyone can be creative, but the spectrum of creative people is vast; what factors determine our place along that spectrum? Environmental conditioning plays a role, genetics may play a limited role, synchronicities play a role, unconscious drives play a major role, and as I mentioned at the end of the previous chapter, the learning we accumulate as the "soul" (the learned propensities of the subtle body) reincarnates through many lifetimes, and may be the most important factor of all.

When the material body dies, these learned tendencies of the subtle body survive as nonlocal memory, and will reincarnate in another physical body in the future. In between death and rebirth, we survive as a "quantum monad" (popularly called a "soul"), a reservoir of accumulated character aspects or propensities that Easterners describe using the Sanskrit words *karma* and *sanskara*.[1]

There is empirical evidence suggesting that memory is nonlocal. In the 1960s the neurophysiologist Karl Lashley set out to find where in the brain we store what we've learned. He trained rats to find cheese in a Y-maze, and then systematically began to remove parts of the rats' brain, testing all the while to see if the learned behavior was eliminated. Strangely, he found that even with 50 percent of its brain removed, a trained rat found its way to the cheese. This finding supports the Vedic idea that learned memory is not only local but also nonlocal, for which the ancient term is *akashic,* a Sanskrit word meaning outside of space and time.

Further relevant empirical evidence can be found in a phenomenon that every parent of a newborn has experienced firsthand. Babies are not born *tabula rasa* (an empty slate) but with already developed propensities that can be triggered. Take the case of the East Indian mathematician Srinivasa Ramanujan, who was born into an entirely nonmathematical family, yet with almost no formal training went on to make extraordinary contributions to mathematical theory, number theory, and infinite series. Then there is the case of Mozart. His family was somewhat musical, but this could hardly explain how as a six-year-old child Wolfgang could compose original scores. To my way of thinking, these geniuses were born with an innate creativity, enhanced by motivation and an ability to focus intention that was passed on to them from their previous incarnations.[2] Victor Hugo was a genius, not simply because he was born with special genetic traits, but because he also brought with him some striking abilities and motivation from past lives.

Yoga Psychology and the Concept of Mental Qualities

Reincarnation theory suggests that of all the propensities we bring from our past reincarnations the three most important are mental qualities known in Sanskrit as *gunas.* The first of these is *tamas.* Tamas, which is Sanskrit for the propensity to act in accord with past conditioning, is ever present; it is a price we pay for growing up and cluttering our brain with memories. Tamas dominates early in our journey of reincarnation; only gradually, after many incarnations, does this tendency give way to *rajas* (Sanskrit for situational creativity) and *sattva* (Sanskrit for fundamental creativity).

The Concept of *dharma*

Each one of us comes to this incarnation with an agenda that Easterners call by its Sanskrit name: *dharma.* To fulfill our dharma, the decree of what we need to learn in this lifetime, we bring with us propensities acquired during many past incarnations. We are not reborn with all of those propensities, however; instead, we bring the particular set that is needed to follow our dharma.

The French mathematician Évariste Galois was killed in a duel at the age of 21; but, even so, he contributed to a new field of mathematics. Young Évariste was schooled at home until age 11, then in high school he studied the great masters of mathematics and began proving mathematical theorems on his own. Most of his work was published posthumously.

What brought Galois to mathematics was a synchronistic encounter with a geometry textbook written by a gifted mathematician. Reading that textbook must have been an unusual experience for Galois, to say the least. Some creativity researchers see this as a crystallizing kind of experience in which a match is made "between a developing person and a particular field of endeavor."[3] From a quantum perspective such moments are a match between one's dharma and a particular field—literally a match made in heaven, because an unconscious drive is involved.

The crystallizing experience is an intuitive awareness of having found your dharma, your way of contributing to a purposeful universe. Joseph Campbell, the famous mythologist, writer, and lecturer, coined the popular phrase "Follow your bliss." He himself had found his bliss early in life by seeking and finding the meaning of myths that derive from the early history of humanity.

My own life-changing experience—the revelation of my dharma—took place in 1973, after having worked as an academic scientist for a decade. I was unhappy, but I did not know why. I was a speaker at a conference in nuclear physics, and when my turn came I gave what I thought was a good presentation. Nevertheless, I was not satisfied; I found myself comparing my presentation with others and feeling jealous, an emotion that persisted throughout the day.

In the evening I was at a party: lots of free food and lots of booze, along with a lot of interesting company and people to impress. But I felt more of the same jealousy. Why were people not paying attention to me, at least not enough attention to relieve my jealous feelings? I realized that I had finished an entire packet of antacid tablets but the heartburn I was suffering from just wouldn't quit.

Feeling desperate, I went outside. The conference was taking place on Monterey Bay in California. It was chilly, so I was alone. Suddenly, as a blast of cool sea breeze hit my face, a thought surfaced, and then repeated itself. "Why do I live this way? Why do I live this way?"

Why was I living in such a way that my professional and personal life had become so totally detached from each other? This question stayed with me, and as time went on it drove me on a quest to integrate physics with my daily life. This, in turn, led to all the things that my life became since then. I had found my dharma!

The discovery of the archetypes with which we identify (lover, mother, father, child, trickster, sage, etc.) requires fundamental creativity. Situational creativity then allows us to engage in many secondary acts of creativity based on that discovery. The more sattva, or fundamental creativity, we have in a particular life, the more we can engage directly with the great archetypes, using creativity "in the search for the soul." If we have sattva along with rajas, or situational creativity, we complement our search for the soul by providing scaffolding for all humanity to evolve.

How do you increase your motivation to be creative? Through what the philosopher Sri Aurobindo called the purification of sattva. Initially, when your sattva is impure, tamas (conditioning) dominates, and all that comes up for unconscious processing is ego stuff and repressed images of the personal unconscious. With the purification of sattva, rajas begins to dominate, and images from the collective unconscious open to you. Only with further purification, with the development of sattva dominance, does your motivation for creativity become driven by the quantum unconscious and become pure curiosity about the archetypes; now you can delve into unconscious processing that takes you into uncharted territory.

Can anyone be creative at this level? Again the answer is yes, but it takes a number of incarnations to build the requisite experience. The fact is that at this stage of human evolution there are many immature souls, for whom creativity will be difficult. If you are interested in creativity, in enhancing the role it can play in shaping your life, then you already have what it takes. Applying a quantum perspective can bring your creative genie (genius?) out of the bottle.

Neuroscientists have discovered that our brain has a remarkable quality called "neuroplasticity"—the ability to lay down new networks of nerve cells to accommodate new learning, including what you learn in support of your deepest creative impulses. You initiate this process by exploring the archetypes, by tuning in to the purposeful universe, by becoming aware of the messages of synchronicity all around you, and most of all by discovering your dharma—your learning agenda.

> You wanna be creative?
> Searching for something
> Some field of exploration
> That matches your dharma?
>
> Expect the unexpected.
> Events of synchronicity
> Will bring you the shoe that fits.
>
> For ever more bliss,
> Purify your sattva.

PART IV

NEW PARADIGMS IN OLD CREATIVE ARENAS

CHAPTER 14

How Cool Is the New Science as a Creative Arena?

The great physicist Richard Feynman said that "scientific imagination is imagination within a straightjacket," although judging by
his accomplishments, Feynman himself never wore one himself. But
many scientists today still think that the advancement of knowledge
depends on the scientific method—a strict application of trial and
error to build theories, which then undergo experimental testing. No
wonder we see such a dearth of creativity and innovation in science
and technology. Fortunately, there is a paradigm shift under way that
recognizes the inadequacy of the scientific method and gives us an
integrative, dogma-free worldview and a proper science of creativity.
The straightjacket is coming off! If you are inclined toward science,
this is the time to consider exploring it. However, brace yourself. The
gale winds of rapid change will continue for years.

Niels Bohr once said about somebody's theory that it was crazy,
but not crazy enough to be right! Any creative solution to a problem
has to be a little crazy to introduce new meaning or open up a new
context. But when the creative idea is crazy enough to shift an entire
paradigm, as is happening now with the primacy of consciousness,
we have to expect a huge amount of resistance. Never forget that
the idea of evolution and the data supporting it have been around

for more than 150 years, yet a substantial number of people in America still don't believe it! Similarly, scientific materialism has very deep roots in our culture. It will take more than a few success stories before the new paradigm gets significant traction.

The old Newtonian physics gave us the themes of causal determinism and objectivity—themes that readily showed themselves in the behavior of macroscopic matter once we learned how to look and analyze, but what really changed society was the industrial revolution that followed. The new quantum physics-based paradigm has brought nonlocality into science, along with the idea of the discontinuity of downward causation. These ideas of nonlocality and discontinuity have already made huge inroads in our vocabulary. Notice how frequently people today invoke the phrase "quantum leap" or talk about their paranormal experiences. Far more importantly, the new science has opened the arena of the subtle body to scientific and technological exploration. This is where the winds of change will create society's eventual acceptance of the new paradigm.

The idea of subtle technology is not entirely new. In the form of what we call "alternative medicine"—Chinese medicine and acupuncture, the Indian medicine of Ayurveda, homeopathy, and so forth—subtle, or vital-energy technology has been around for millennia. Whereas the cost of modern allopathic medicine is going up everywhere by leaps and bounds, alternative medicine is cheap by comparison. Also, alternative medicine is preventive, and has no side effects to speak of; compared to allopathic medicine, this is a huge boon. Alternative medicine works best for chronic disease, which becomes more prevalent for most people as they grow old. Imagine how wonderful it would be to get medicine for an ailment at an older age without worrying about side effects! And here is the especially good news for creative people: If any field needs new research and creative exploration, it is alternative medicine, with its vast, largely untapped potential.

We can see the beginnings of a science of measurement of vital energy in the form of Kirlian photography, which uses electrophysiological fields at the skin to measure the nonlocally correlated vital energies. New measurement devices using photons emitted by our organs (biophoton emission) are well under way, providing another huge arena for creativity. No genius is required to tell us that vital energy technology is the new frontier of technology in the 21st century.

Some of the new technology will center on restoration. We have made gross mistakes in the recent past with growing grains in genetically modified fashion, using harsh chemicals for treating the soil, thinning the ozone layer, and poisoning our water, our oceans, and our air. All these things certainly affect vital energies that have to be restored. But the most important vital energy technologies of the future will come as surprises, for that is the nature of creativity.

Just for fun I will share with you two of my own futuristic scenarios. A couple is fighting with gusto. Suddenly, the woman says, "I need a break." The woman then goes to her bedroom and spreads a perfume vitalized with energy from the heart chakra on herself. When she goes back into the room, her partner suddenly becomes very respectful, empathic, loving, and open to seeing the other side of the issue. Imagine what that heart-chakra perfume could accomplish at the United Nations!

The other scenario that goes through my mind sometimes is that of a business agreement about to be signed, or a peace treaty, or a proposal of marriage. And as a matter of course all involved take out their handheld biophoton tomography machines and hold them in front of each other's heart chakras to gauge how much love they're emitting.

The Future of Science

I predict that as our society increasingly recognizes a new science based on the primacy of consciousness, what we call "big science" will vanish from the scene. Big science deals with expensive research for projects that have very little to do with the human condition. Examples are space exploration projects and big particle accelerators. By and large, these projects have been boondoggles (except for their contributions to weapons research—the source of their political support), while for some time it has been clear that no government on earth has enough money to support these big items. Now that we can see that the emperor of scientific materialism has no clothes, we can make peace with the fact that his grandiose promises will never be fulfilled.

As we integrate alternative medicine into the mainstream and start using preventive medicine in a major way, the big pharmaceutical companies will lose their grip on the medical practice, and chemistry will lose much of its appeal as a creative opportunity. While physics and chemistry may wane in creative importance, there will still be scope for technological innovations in these fields as they contribute to ever-important engineering.

The life sciences will be the big winner in the new paradigm, however, but not in a big-ticket way like the human genome project. The emphasis will be on subtle energy, on consciousness studies that require the participation of creative human beings more than big expensive machinery. Human capital will be a big part of the new economy. Bioengineering will advance hand in hand with vital energy technology. Psychology will become integrated as we use primacy-of-consciousness metaphysics to guide us. This will enable us to make huge creative investments in the service of positive bodily and mental health.

A Dialog with a Young Scientist

Young Scientist: Okay, I recognize the huge scope of creativity in the new science. But isn't it true though that paradigm shifters and extenders in science are always that rare breed called geniuses? Don't ordinary scientists who are not so gifted just plod along?

Author: Not true. The Nobel laureate physicist Paul Dirac once said that during the quantum revolution in physics in the 1920s, even second-rate physicists did first-rate work. I think what he meant is that during a paradigm shift, many more scientists make creative contributions simply because of the availability of a great many tractable problems that need solutions. When a new paradigm appears on the scene, there is no big repertoire of known contexts and meanings from which to draw. And so even "ordinary" scientists have to engage creatively.

Young Scientist: Isn't it the case that paradigm shifts are rare in the history of individual fields of science? So what if there is no paradigm shift going on in a given field? Should young people like me stay away from it?

Author: In times of stable paradigms, even first-rate sophisticated scientists are reduced to working on second-rate problems that require only mechanistic solutions. Should we therefore discourage them from making science their primary enterprise during times of stable paradigms? Is that your question?

Young Scientist: I guess that is what I am asking. After all your encouragement to engage in creativity, wouldn't it be a shame to get bogged down if there is no new paradigm on the horizon, no scope for that creativity? Maybe creative young people should concentrate more on the arts, or try their hands at business, leaving science to the mechanical problem solvers.

Author: There's no need for pessimism. Certainly, when a paradigm is on the decline, we have a tendency to specialize in order to make a contribution. But you still can get creative juices flowing by allowing quantum thinking to address a given problem, no matter how practical or mundane it may seem. Moreover, there is always the possibility that a new paradigm is coming around the corner much the way the new model based on consciousness has.

Young Scientist: I don't see too many people flocking toward consciousness studies either. Science is too specialized and the field of consciousness studies is too interdisciplinary for most scientists.

Author: Those who depend on their intuition—and most creative people do—will find a way to gravitate to wherever the creative action is, even if it means going outside their field.

Young Scientist: And there is also, for us young people, the awkward question of financial support.

Author: True. The ubiquitous power of economics. It is true that most scientists who have a lot of grant support tend to emphasize the status quo. I'm paraphrasing, but novelist Upton Sinclair said it's difficult to make a man understand something when his salary depends on his not understanding it.

Still, practitioners of the old paradigm will be stuck if young people refuse to join them in their business-as-usual. In the '60s, many young people stepped out of the rat race, and some of them never returned. But they triggered a revolution in the academy, a liberalization of attitudes. After all, what would the movers and shakers do without creative people? If the able and the intelligent insist on creative opportunities, society must respond.

Young Scientist: It's easy for you to say. You come from a country where material needs are underemphasized. In this country, materialism still holds the reins. In this economy we accept a good job even if it means inane, repetitive work.

Author: Never compromise your creative freedom. If your livelihood doesn't encourage creativity, change it. That's where you have to draw the line, at least in economically advanced countries. Hold out, meditate, be open to the creative opportunity for exploring meaning and it will come.

Young Scientist: Okay. Say for the sake of argument that I eventually land a job in a great research lab doing consciousness research. The problem of dealing with a vast hierarchy remains. There will always be people telling me what to do—and what not to do. What's true for materialist science also will be true for consciousness research.

Author: But do you really have to comply? Listen to the advice of physicist and Nobel laureate Isidor Rabi:

> We don't teach our students enough of the intellectual content of experiments—their novelty and their capacity for opening new fields. . . . My own view is that you take these things personally. You do an experiment because your own philosophy makes you want to know the result. It's too hard, and life is too short, to spend your time doing something because someone else has said it's important. You must feel the thing yourself.[1]

If you don't feel that a certain question is worth investigating, don't do it. Period. Have you ever tried not compromising your freedom? There are subtle movements of consciousness, synchronicities that step in to help us when we do. We are not alone in our striving for creative freedom.

Young Scientist: Okay. So let's say that the lab director lets me carry out my own novel experiment. But creative work takes enormous time. My publications dwindle. In the current economic model for scientific activity I am no longer satisfying the criterion of excellence. I don't have tenure, so I get fired. What good does that do me, or anyone else?

Author: Good point. The new paradigm is going to change things in ways we can't predict, and eventually success will be measured differently, I believe. In the meantime remember to work on some conventional stuff on the side, be helpful to others, that kind of thing. Until you get tenure.

Young Scientist: Even tenured professors aren't given raises if they don't produce, or if their work doesn't earn their peers' approval. What if the new economic model fails to gain ground for a long time?

Author: That's the risk you have to take. If you do, you will find that it is worth it. You will be happier living with yourself. Creativity is its own reward, which may sound trite because it is so often repeated, but it is still true. Meanwhile, as a society we must change. We must allow young scientists to devote time to pursuing burning questions. We need to achieve more balance between fundamental and situational creativity and between creativity and mechanical problem solving. Science and society need them all.

Young Scientist: I wish the movers and shakers would hear you.

Author: They will. They're already beginning to. They don't live outside consciousness. No one does. And as we get further into this new era of science within consciousness, there will be unprecedented opportunity for creativity, both fundamental and situational.

Young Scientist: Ah, science within consciousness. Do you anticipate that when we include the subjective in science, then how we do science will also change?

Author: I'm glad you asked. To this point science has been shackled by its efforts to be objective—except for moments of extraordinary creativity, which have always been subjective. But even so, within the Newtonian paradigm scientists tried taking themselves out of the equation in the name of objectivity. The demands of science within consciousness—idealist science—will be quite different. The idealist scientist must be prepared to let consciousness transform him or her during the process of investigation. After all, the scientific quest for truth is a hero's journey, a very powerful archetype for transformation.

Young Scientist: What do you mean, transformation? You are not suggesting that we all become spiritual practitioners of inner creativity, are you?

Author: It seems to be inevitable for the truly great scientists. Listen to what the authors Willis Harman and Christian de Quincey have to say about this:

> The point is that the transformation in experience which the scientist would undergo while exploring consciousness is essential for the kind of direct and deep insight required to gain knowledge of the psyche. Without that, the scientist would be blind to the phenomena and processes under investigation. Such "inner vision" is the starting point—the *sine qua non*—of any true consciousness science; it is the source of data which, later, the scientist can build into a communicable model.[2]

Do you understand?

Young Scientist: I never thought about it this way before, but I think I do. It's exciting.

Author: Let me emphasize one more thing. Even if you are engaged in tasks that require only mechanical problem solving, there is one way to transform them into creativity. You can do this by using problem solving to serve the world—humanity and its environment. Action in the service of others always touches the quantum self—it is inner creativity at its purest, and it will even transform you in the process. There is no better incentive for action.

The idea of Einstein's space
Is beyond Einstein's space.
The laws of Newton are not written
On the bodies they govern.

Ideas and laws, oh creative,
Are your transcendent companions in potentia
Waiting for you; they are attracted to you.

Earthbound, scientists may be,
But when they discover the laws of nature,
Responding to heavenly attraction,
They soar in heaven.
Problem solving is efficient, to be sure,
But don't you wish to mount the quantum catapult
Just once? Your own encounter
With this new context, consciousness,
This new meaning of science,
Will launch you too into heaven.

CHAPTER 15

Reviving the Arts

I have said before that creativity in the arts—poetry, literature, music, theater, dance, philosophy, painting, sculpture, architecture—all have suffered or have been sidetracked with the advent of scientific materialism. Its practitioners stay within the self-imposed straight-jacket of scientific materialism (now you see why the abbreviation SM is apt); they never quantum leap to the archetypal realm, with its endless connection to the deeper truths that connect us all. Then the post-modern philosophy of existentialism—existence precedes essence—influences the arts by making them morose and pessimistic.

But as science brings us a new worldview centered on consciousness, vitality, meaning, and values, the arts will revive. Let's look at some differences between the sciences and the arts to get an appreciation of the task ahead.

Paradigm Shifts in the Arts

The fundamental feature of a paradigm shift is discontinuity—the illogical, nonlinear gap between the old paradigm and the new. Some aspects of the old paradigm may remain useful, but after a shift we can never look at the old in the same old way. The new context reshapes our understanding of truth.

Science is progressive in the sense that new laws replace old ones. The validity of the old laws, although still functional in the old arena (an idea known as the correspondence principle), is only approximate.

In contrast, in the arts, be it painting, music, or literature, the old and new paradigms coexist peacefully, each in its own right. For example, Picasso initiated the new paradigm of cubism, depicting an object from different perspectives in the same piece of art. This new paradigm reflects the multidimensionality of 20th-century culture and forever changes the way we appreciate all art, present and past, but it doesn't diminish our appreciation of what came before.

Until the 20th century in the West, dance consisted only of folk dance and classical ballet. When Martha Graham developed a new paradigm in the late 1920s, modern dance, she broke with tradition to introduce a new context. But modern dance did not affect our appreciation of either ballet or folk forms. In her own words: "Once we strove to imitate gods—we did god dances. Then we strove to become part of nature by representing natural forces in dance forms—winds—flowers—trees. . . . [Modern dance] was not done perversely to dramatize ugliness or to strike at sacred tradition. . . . There was a revolt against the ornamental forms of impressionistic dancing."

Science is progressive also in Newton's sense of seeing "so much because I could stand on the shoulders of giants." In the arts, strictly speaking, there is no need to stand on the shoulders of giants. Yes, they can teach us technique, but how that technique is applied to capture the meaning of an archetypal theme depends entirely on the artist. As Gertrude Stein said, "What is seen depends upon how everybody is doing everything."

Originality in the Arts

In one episode of the comic strip *Calvin and Hobbes,* Calvin says to Hobbes, "The problem with fine arts is that it's supposed to express original truths. But who wants originality and truth?" he complains. "People want more of what they already know they like." Does Calvin have a point?

Many scientists look upon science as a professional enterprise and embark on career science, using the scientific method for their problem solving, cluttering up the scientific journals. Even artists could use the scientific method to write a poem, or draw a painting. If one were interested in art as a professional problem, staying confined in the straightjacket of SM, then they might take the following steps to "scientifically" write a poem:

1. Find a worthwhile subject (the problem).

2. Produce a few ideas to proceed; they don't have to be original. Unabashedly draw on some of your favorite poems for starters.

3. Do it! Produce a poem following each of your ideas.

4. Decide which one works best.

5. Integrate the best of the other versions into your best choice. Of course, you don't conduct experiments to verify the value of a poem, but you do test it out in the public arena. If people like it, you have succeeded.

Thousands of poems and pop music lyrics seem to be written this way every year. And the same method should work in other arts with a little modification. However, be aware that although we do like the familiar comfort of encountering what we already know, few of us would call movie sequels, TV soap operas, Harlequin romances, and teen series books creative art. Poet Robert Graves spoke of shivers in the spine when writing a poem; others describe palpitations in the heart and feelings of intoxication. If you opt for the scientific method to write a poem, you will never experience such sensations.

Novelist Jack Kerouac saw writing as part of a battle against conformity, as did Allen Ginsberg and other members of the Beat Generation, and by doing so they created a new movement in American poetry. "We were writing for our own amusement and the amusement of our friends, rather than for money or for publication," Ginsberg once said in an interview.

Unlike the sciences, the discovery of new themes, new truths, is not the goal in the arts—that is, the originality of artists does not lie in the uniqueness of the truth or themes they express. Original art throughout the ages has reveled in the same transcendent themes—love, beauty, justice, etc. These themes are so profound that no one artist can ever express them completely; they remain original forever. The challenge to the artist in exploring "new truth" is to build a bridge between eternal themes and the specific context of a particular place and time. As author John Briggs put it, "So though the 'truth' . . . for Homer, Cervantes, Balzac or Faulkner may be at some level the same, evidently that truth must be constantly remade through different historical contexts—so it is many different truths as well."

Even good postmodern art, whose avowed motif is to "deconstruct," ends up pointing us to the transcendental nature of all truth. Postmodern pessimism signaled the end of the societal euphoria of the industrial age, which put too much emphasis on material progress. Fundamental creativity in the arts—the discovery of new paradigms or a radical extension of the old one—goes one step further. There are artists who are way ahead of their time, who anticipate socio-cultural change that has not yet broken through the inertia of the commonplace. This is the arena of Homer, Kalidasa, Shakespeare, Michelangelo, Bach, Dostoyevsky, Picasso, van Gogh, Rabindranath Tagore, Martha Graham, and the Beatles, to name just a few. Being ahead of their time is one reason we find so many cases of great artists overlooked by their contemporaries (van Gogh being just one tragic example). But the artist who has heard the siren song of creativity has to take the risk that others just won't understand their work.

This risk-taking separates the wheat from the chaff, creativity from mechanical problem solving. In a conversation with writer John Hyde Preston, Gertrude Stein said of the originality of American novelists: "You will write . . . if you will write without thinking of the result in terms of a result, but think of the writing in terms of discovery, which is to say that creation must take place between the pen and the paper, not before in a thought or afterwards in a recasting."

Most people in the arts, however, engage in less risky activities, working within the parameters of a well-defined paradigm. But popular art can be creative, too. So long as artists are not using calculated steps that can be anticipated (canned poetry, formulaic movies, or art as problem solving), they are still engaging in creativity, quantum-style; they still confront the risky possibility that they will not succeed in creating a bridge between their audience and a timeless truth.

Professionalism in the arts, as essential as it is, tends to breed mediocrity. Professionals have to produce a certain number of successes in order to maintain their professional standing. Also, professionals breed more professionals through writing schools, poetry conferences, and the process of publishing itself. It's not all bad, but creativity can suffer, as the critic John Aldridge notes about the contemporary American writing scene:

> What is at issue here is a professional fraternity so obsessed with turning out writers that it has lost all regard for the purpose they are supposed to serve and the skill with which they are expected to serve it. It is rather as if the medical profession were to produce physicians whose ability to treat patients is considered irrelevant when weighed against the fact that the medical profession must be kept going and that the training of physicians is a vital source of revenue and prestige.[1]

Most importantly, many professional American writers have lost sight of the primary law of creativity: grand vision. Consider John Dos Passos's *U.S.A. Trilogy* or Norman Mailer's *An American Dream.* In the first, the author describes the destruction of transcendent values in modern American culture; in the second, the archetypal battle between good and evil is played out in New York City. These stories have a vision ambitious enough to explore original truths. There is little equivalent on the current American writing scene, with a few exceptions, such as the work of Toni Morrison and Alice Walker. We're more likely to find a new context in the South American works of such powerful writers as Gabriel Garcia Marquez (author of the Nobel-winning *One Hundred Years of Solitude*) and Isabel Allende.

If the joy of creativity is what attracts one to the arts, how can one not notice that the joy dries up in projects that require only reason? How can the artist turn from the encounter with the quantum self—"the flute of interior time," as the Sufi poet Kabir put it—once she has heard its call?

Artist-poet Carolyn Kleefeld says, "Most artists are like engineers reproducing the familiar. This type of art, from the outside in, is not the same art as art that is being created as part of an emerging consciousness."

Novelist D. H. Lawrence reminds us of the necessity for creativity with these powerful words:

> Man fixes some wonderful erection of his own between himself and the wild chaos, and gradually goes bleached and stiffened under his parasol. Then comes a poet, enemy of convention, and makes a slit in the umbrella; and lo! the glimpse of chaos is a vision, a window to the sun.[2]

No Apologies Needed: Dialog with an Artist

Artist: I thank you on behalf of all artists for elevating the creativity in the arts to the same level as the creativity in science. I feel relevant again.

Author: One of the most devastating consequences of the materialist worldview is the loss of relevance of the arts and humanities. The fact that a few creatives still pursue fine arts, engage in serious painting, write poems, create sculpture, and write real literature, is a testimony to the power of the archetypes; they motivate us.

Artist: We put a face to them, but feel indulgent doing something that the mainstream considers irrelevant!

Author: Look, the worldview is shifting. Make no mistake about it. In the new worldview the value of all archetypes is acknowledged; not only the archetype of truth (or the sage) that science pursues, but also love (or the lover), justice, the trickster, and others that turn the artist on. No apologies are needed. But we do need you to be activists.

Artist: What do you mean?

Author: It will take a while to fully change the paradigm; scientific materialism is still very entrenched. The media, and many people in positions of power, are sold on it.

Artist: Yes, I noticed. Most politicians who call themselves liberals are atheists, based on their entrenchment in scientific materialism. On the other hand, conservatives side with Christian fundamentalists who aren't big on creative expression. Who can an artist turn to?

Author: And it doesn't help that the media has been taught to report in a value-free way. Beauty must be balanced by ugliness, right by wrong, good by evil, and all must get equal time in the media. The criterion for judging is no longer value, but fame.

Artist: So you propose activism. What do want us to do exactly?

Author: You have to educate your audience. You yourselves not only have to engage in quantum thinking but also publicize its importance, and even teach others to think that way. It should be easy for you. All highly creative people live a quantum lifestyle anyway. Your job is to make it more explicit and persuade others to approve this quantum lifestyle.

> Professional or amateur—neither
> Is sufficient for creativity.
> You must embrace responsibility, Oh creative.
> Do not stop short of the goal as amateurs often do.
> And forswear the self-limiting of the ego's career needs;
> They too often dominate the professional's drive.
> Rather, heed your quantum self! It speaks through your intuition
> Whenever ego-you is in abeyance.
>
> Here, now, the whole, all at once,
> You never thought you could write it down, did you?
>
> But you are a professional. The eternal archetypes
> Bloom anew in the fresh forms you discover to clothe
> The ever-changing context of your again-new age.
>
> Like an amateur, you move on
> From context to context, from meaning to meaning,
> Ever ranging ahead of your professional self.

CHAPTER 16

How Can One Be Creative in Business?

Many businesses begin with an act of creativity—somebody's innovative new idea for a product or a service. And as everybody knows, no innovation is forever. New ideas replace old ones; innovations start new trends. Paradigms shift in science and technology, and our societies change worldviews—and businesses have to reflect those changes. All of this requires creativity on an ongoing basis.

Organizations require structures and hierarchies, and rely on past experience to avoid chaos. This requires a lot of training as well. Creativity and conditioning; businesses need both, which is not unlike balancing yang and yin in Chinese medicine. Understanding the nature of creativity and conditioning is essential for achieving balance. But there is much more than that going on right now.

The need for new paradigm thinking is coming to business. Not long ago, environmental pollution by business and industry was accepted as a necessary evil to achieve growth and job creation. Business was satisfied with the assumption of infinite resources, on which the current materialist economic paradigm is based. So what prompted business to look for alternatives? The arrival of two undeniable emergencies: global climate change (a direct effect of environmental pollution) and the soaring price of oil, leading to increased production costs for virtually all businesses. Now increasingly the business conversation has shifted to eco-friendliness and sustainability. The next step is to see that sustainability is not possible within the materialist arena. Businesses have to extend their creativity into the subtle arena of human experience.

Creativity in Business and the Subtle

Business knows the importance of the subtle. For example, a customer chooses a product based not only on an objective appraisal of its uses but also how he or she feels about it. The fact is that the subtle, working as it does on the level of emotions, hunches, and intuition, influences the gross; there is no way around it. And business has always been tuned in to this fact. Look at car ads, for example. If consumer considerations for buying a car were purely logical, ads would focus exclusively on gas mileage, reliability, and maintenance costs. Instead most ads talk about fun, power, speed, and make direct or indirect references to the car's sex appeal. Many businesses, the auto industry among them, try to sell their product by appealing to the lower chakras, whose energy is responsible for feeling grounded, and for sexuality and self-confidence.

But the human condition is not limited to the lower chakras; there are also higher chakras starting with the heart, where the movement of vital energy can give rise to love, self-expression, wisdom, and spiritual connection. We're constantly being reminded that it's a dog-eat-dog world as far as business is concerned, but this lower-chakra business paradigm shows signs of shifting. When the Japanese way of running production lines (in which a worker is responsible for a finished product) became popular, along with the slogan "quality is job one," businesses worldwide recognized the importance of the job satisfaction that an employee derives from seeing his or her handiwork. There is a place for higher emotion in business after all!

In the consciousness-based worldview we acknowledge that creativity consists of discoveries or inventions of new meaning that contain value. In business this means we don't have to give up profit as a motive, but it takes a secondary role. From low-wattage electric bulbs to social media, new businesses find value in contributing—directly or indirectly—to our capacity for processing meaning. Profit is a by-product of that value.

As we've seen all too vividly in the Great Recession, one of the evils of business today is the rise of the financial institutions whose only product is the manipulation of money. This is not a desirable trend because there is no creativity involved; these businesses add nothing of intrinsic value because money has no intrinsic value. But it does represent the promise of power. That people even consider—much less train for—entering a business based on the manipulation of money is a symptom of the deterioration of values in life under a materialist worldview. Like legalized gambling, making money speculating on money needs to be tightly regulated.

On the positive side, over the long term, consciousness is always evolving toward making the processing of meaning accessible to more and more people. When your business adds a meaningful product or service to your society and environment, it is attuned to the evolutionary movement of consciousness. When this happens, your intention (in this case to have a successful creative business) is backed by the full power of nonlocal quantum consciousness.

So remember that in terms of consciousness, there are two important purposes for your business, whatever it may be: First, your business must disseminate positive emotion and meaning-processing to people. When this purpose is clearly expressed through your business dealings, you cannot fail. The invisible hands of the free market, the movement of consciousness itself, will come to your aid. Second, to attune yourself and your business to other people's positive feelings and meanings you have to engage in business not with the exclusive purpose of making money, but with the idea of exploring the archetype of abundance. Abundance is not just about material wealth; it includes meaning, higher emotions like satisfaction, and spiritual growth. You cannot pursue abundance with a closed heart; the two are antithetical.

How to Begin a Creative Business

There is an unforgettable idea in the movie *Field of Dreams:* When the field is ready, people will come. This is true of business, too. All you need is faith in the quantum possibilities of your psyche—and your ability to harness them. The co-founders of Apple Inc., Steve Jobs and Steve Wozniak, consulted with lawyers and venture capitalists about starting a business without knowing exactly what they were setting up. Strangely, this openness was crucial to the entity they eventually established. In the same vein, Paul Cook, a founder of the Raychem Corporation, said, "When we started, we didn't know what we're going to do. We didn't know what products we were going to make."

In this aspect, creativity in business is no different from all other expressions of creativity: They begin with questions, not answers. For example, an important question is, Can I make life more meaningful through establishing this business enterprise—contributing meaning for myself, my employees, and for the people who use my product (or service)? Contrary to common sense, creative businesses begin with the seed of an idea—an intuition, a field of possibilities open to the new.

Being in Business

In the 1954 movie *Executive Suite,* a struggle takes place between a conservative "bean counter" type who wants to stay the course, without any interest in risk or creativity, and a visionary who's pushing for creative change or bust. The adventurer wins the executive suite and the business is able to continue as a dynamic creative entity, changing as the movement of consciousness demands it. Taking no risks is certainly a recipe for disaster, but willingness to take chances and a vision are not enough. Preparing the field for planting is a good beginning, but the next step is to take on a process to manifest from the field of possibilities products that will improve the quality of people's lives. Only then will consumers come.

Businesspeople are ostensibly always on the run, with a deep need to be in control all the time, but these stereotypes miss the mark when it comes to creative businesspeople. One of the great developments of our time is the emergence of a popular antidote to the anxious mind—the relaxation response. To learn to relax is to learn to be in your own company without judgment, and without incessantly creating the past or the future. The creative businessman is an expert in living this way—being fully in the moment. Stanford University professors Michael Ray and Rochelle Myers wrote a book, *Creativity in Business,* in which they quote Robert Marcus of Alumax, famous in the 1980s for his business acumen.

> We're an efficient company in terms of people per dollar. Although we're a two-billion-dollar company, we have only eighty-four people in headquarters. Which isn't too many. We're doing the same thing, but we're not as big as Alcoa or Alcan. We're about a third of their size, but we have a tenth of the number of people in headquarters. It seems to work pretty well, so we're going to stick with it. . . .
>
> I'll tell you some of the things we do. We don't have a lot of meetings. We don't write a lot of reports. We make quick decisions. You know, if it takes you a long time to make decisions, if you have a lot of meetings and write a lot of reports, you need a lot of people. We communicate very rapidly. We do it all by word of mouth. I don't write letters. I don't write reports. In fact, I don't know what I do. . . . We play squash often. . . .
>
> I don't let time I allocate to some big parts of my life interfere with each other. I confine my business time, which is pretty much nine-to-five. . . . I go out to play [squash] three times a week. And I don't feel really pressed by business.[1]

This creative businessman learned to relax; he developed a sense of equanimity about time. He learned to complement the conventional do-do-do of the business mind with an awareness of the importance of just being. By unconsciously processing many possibilities at the same time, being complements doing. And this is the secret of creativity.

Another way of putting this was beautifully expressed by author Rochelle Myers, who suggested revising the adage "Don't just stand there, do something," so that its advice is more in keeping with quantum creativity: "Don't just do something, stand there."

The Creative Process in Business: Do-Be-Do-Be-Do

Do all businesspeople need to follow the do-be-do-be-do mantra of creativity? To quote Robert Marcus again, "Always make sure you do the important things and do them well. And allow enough time for them." This is the trick—making enough time for a job allows do-be-do-be-do and enables creativity. This insight in itself is a quantum leap, a discontinuous thought that brings both surprise and certainty. Once you see that a process that includes being relaxed about your business actually produces better decisions, it becomes easier to trust non-doing.

Big insights give businesses their big breakthrough products: start-up ideas like the internal combustion engine, or more recently, an Internet search engine called Google. For an established business, though, it is the little quantum leaps of everyday business activities that keep the business running smoothly. When do-be-do-be-do is incorporated into the modus operandi, the gap between doing and being shrinks so much that the shift from one to the other becomes hardly noticeable. And if being comes with a sense of surrender in which the doer refuses to resolve the usual conflicts of work with business's three worst enemies—thinking too big, too small, and too much—something special happens. The sense of a doer disappears, and the doing seems to happen by itself.

This effortless creative action is flow. When one achieves this way of doing business, work itself becomes pleasure.

Collective Creativity: Brainstorming

So far we have only spoken of individual creativity, which is certainly a cornerstone of business success. However, in a business often an entire group works together toward a creative product. How does one apply do-be-do-be-do to collective creativity? One traditional way is brainstorming, but I suggest that this approach is ineffective—at least the way it is usually practiced.

In conventional brainstorming, people sit around a table and share their thoughts on the problem at hand. The basic instructions are openness and tolerance: no comment is too dumb to be shared, and everyone should try to listen without passing judgment. The idea here is that the power of divergent thinking will prevail through brainstorming and lead the group to a solution. From the quantum creativity point of view, however, divergent thinking at the conscious level only leads to more ideas from the known, and we can never access the unknown that way. What we need is a divergence of meaning processing in our *unconscious* that invites new possibilities.

This can be achieved in brainstorming by engaging the art of listening not only without judgment but also with the addition of internal silence. One should express and share, of course, not from the busy mind but from being itself. And the participants must allow conflict to be processed in the unconscious; they have to keep conflicting ideas in focus and yet not try to resolve all their differences with continuous and rational ideas. This is practicing do-be-do-be-do with conflict. Conflict is important because it enlarges the space of unconscious processing to include new possibilities. Eventually, a quantum leap will bring the new insight through one or more people of the group.

Changing Current Big Business Practices: The Economics of Consciousness

Whereas creativity tends to thrive in small businesses and start-ups, the story is quite different for big business corporations. For such enterprises the objective of business is to amass power and to dominate others. Today some multinational corporations have amassed more power than many nation-states.

How did it get this way? To make a long story short, the capitalism of economist Adam Smith has undergone many changes that make it a very different beast. Smith envisioned that in a free-market economy equilibrium would be established between production and consumption; prices would stabilize and resources would be allocated properly. However, Smith's capitalist economy suffers from periodic recession and subsequent inflationary expansion—the business cycle of boom and bust.

When recession hits, government intervention is needed to lead the economy in recovery. Monetary policy controls the money supply to keep a check on inflation. Originally, government intervention took place according to the ideas of economist John Maynard Keynes: government would put people to work through investment in infrastructure, often by borrowing money—that is, deficit financing—allowing time for a business to regroup. But in the 1980s, partly because of the oil crisis and partly because of misuse of Keynesian economics, a situation called stagflation arose, in which decreasing business activity and rapid inflation took place at the same time. With stagflation, the Keynesian solution of increasing employment through government spending becomes problematic since that would certainly throw gas on the flames of inflation.

Economists found a solution called supply-side economics that tries to solve the problem by increasing money supply without creating demand. One example of this is cutting taxes for the rich (again, often using deficit financing), putting money in the pockets of people who will then invest in business, which will create jobs so money will "trickle down" to ordinary people.

The downside here is that this system is also unstable. As it turns out, one consequence of supply-side economics is that the rich get richer and the poor get poorer, creating a huge wealth gap, and with it political instability. As the middle class shrinks in size the amount of creativity in the society as a whole goes down—an altogether antievolutionary dynamic. There is a limit to how far we can go with deficit financing without producing problems. The limitations on natural resources and the problem of increased environmental pollution create further instability. Additionally, these models assume that consumer and business behavior can be predicted. As we've discovered, this is far from the truth, since labile emotions and herd mentality continue to influence how people invest and spend their money.

In 2007 and 2008, a combination of these and other factors produced a huge recession, an economic meltdown that has made the validity of revising Adam Smith's capitalism less than appetizing.

Furthermore, multinationals and the growth of corporate power were a direct product of the change in economic policy. The rich did not invest in supplying venture capital and creating new small businesses that would have fostered creativity. Instead, they saw an opportunity in already big corporations that benefited from tax loopholes and outsourced labor. Many of the new multimillionaires and multibillionaires invested their wealth in speculation and financial sleight of hand.

Can we bring creativity into the operation of big corporations and multinationals? Can we solve the instability of boom-bust cycles without supply-side or demand-side deficit financing? We can. A fundamental shortcoming of the capitalism that emerged in the 18th century as a replacement for feudal and mercantile economies is that it confined itself only to the material balance sheet of business enterprises to meet people's needs. But as Abraham Maslow has noted, people have an entire hierarchy of needs—not only material but also subtle. Subtle needs create demand for subtle products that enhance or develop vital energies, and the exploration of meaning, beauty, love, and truth. These needs are partially met right now by spiritual enterprises like churches, humanistic endeavors like teaching institutions, artistic enterprises in the form of art galleries and museums, and the businesses of alternative medicine. These enterprises may not function as part of the free market today, but they could certainly be redesigned to do so.

Entities that deal in the subtle create products whose value therefore cannot be based on material benefit alone. Additionally, now that the scientific know-how is here, business enterprises that deal with material products may feel encouraged to include subtle components as well. Thus a more inclusive economics that redresses the imbalance between the subtle and the gross is needed. Such an economics is being developed, and the good news is that it solves the problem of boom-bust cycles without introducing the evils of demand- or supply-side economics.

The basic idea of such an economics is to include the subtle in the hierarchy of people's needs that business should strive to satisfy, using the gifts of creative people who explore the subtle. The objective of economics is the creation of wealth; the archetype to pursue is abundance. Clearly, there is infinite abundance in the subtle domain, and its inclusion can be a boon to economics.

Creativity in Big Businesses under the Economics of Consciousness

In the documentary *Corporation,* the filmmakers demonstrate that modern corporations display all the symptoms of psychopathic behavior. Converting to the economics of consciousness means making a dramatic shift in how business is run. A business is no longer an organization with one bottom line—material profit. Now it can be explicitly recognized that:

1. The production of subtle products also has value.

2. Labor can be paid not only in terms of material remuneration but also in terms of the subtle—by the gift of more leisure time, for example, or a meditation break during work hours, the company of spiritual masters, and so forth.

3. With labor expenses controlled in this way, outsourcing can be considerably reduced and meaningful employment can be restored to economically advanced countries.

4. Meaningful jobs can also be created in the subtle sectors of the economy, to which corporations themselves may contribute directly or indirectly. If the corporation deals with organic products, this is an example of a direct contribution to the vital energy economy; hiring consultants to improve the mental health of employees is an example of an indirect contribution.

5. Outsourcing opens the door and subtle economy restores meaning-processing in economically advanced countries, opening them up to new realms of creativity.

6. Big business can take further advantage of its creative
    labor force by including it in quality production, in
    research, and in other creative activities as much as
    practicable. In this way the corporation itself becomes
    creative. When big business becomes a producer
    of positive subtle energy—even indirectly through
    increased employee job satisfaction—the whole society
    gets a creativity boost.[2]

Will this development affect developing countries adversely? Not
necessarily. Don't forget that developing countries also need to convert to the economics of consciousness. So long as attention is given
to this shift, developing economies will become less dependent on
the relatively meaningless jobs provided by outsourcing.

Creativity with Love: Eco-friendliness in Businesses

When businesses adopt the economics of consciousness, green
business policies follow automatically, and many businesses are becoming aware that green business policies do not necessarily lead
to red bottom lines. Another great advantage of the economics of
consciousness over the current materialist economics is that we will
no longer have to depend on consumerism to drive the economy.
This means that we can reduce our consumption of nonrenewable
resources and our production of environmental pollution, reducing
global climate change in a major way.

The economics of consciousness allows our societies a less hurried
lifestyle that is highly conducive to creativity, providing an unprecedented quality of life. This in turn will reduce people's dependence
on material pleasure as a substitute for happiness. In this way we will
move away from the unsustainable material standard of living currently in vogue. Many of these reduced material requirements will be
provided by renewable sources of energy at our disposal.

The possibilities are unlimited. In this map of our future that we
envision, creativity is the means. Can we be creative in business? We

can and we must, in order to implement the paradigm shift in economics that is aborning.

Economics and economic laws
Lay hidden in the night.
(Feudalism prevailed: few rich, many poor.
And hardly anybody processed meaning.)
God said, "Let Adam Smith be,"
And there was light.
(Middle class, meaning-processing, age of enlightenment!)
It did not last; materialism shouted, "Ho."
Materialist economics, supply-side voodoo,
Speculation, derivatives
Restored the status quo.
(Back to the dark ages: few rich, many poor;
Shrinking middle class, little meaning-processing, littler creativity.)
God said, "Here's quantum physics and the economics of consciousness,
Recognize the dynamic duo."
(And the middle class, meaning, and creativity
Will be back again in the saddle.)

CHAPTER 17

Toward a Creative Society

When we look at the world today, it's difficult to see much beyond polarization. Because so many creative people have been misled into accepting scientific materialism, they try to express their creativity while wearing the straightjacket of a belief system in which creativity, indeed, consciousness itself and all its values, are impossible. People's creativity suffers because its success requires quantum processing, which is incompatible with the frenetic lifestyle of materialism, with its tendency to rely on the rational mind. Another segment of society sees this approach as wrong—often due to strong religious convictions—but these people too are misled by a religious conservatism that is based on outmoded ways of seeing the world, including the place of women. Because of their archaic belief system, they, too, are suspicious of creativity.

This resistance from both camps has made it difficult to develop creative solutions to problems of crisis proportions that we must solve: global climate change, terrorism, economic meltdowns, the breakdown of democracy, moribund religions, regressive education, and skyrocketing health care costs. We cannot successfully address these problems without transforming our divisive approach into an integrative worldview.

Look at how silly some of the games are that these polarized people play. Materialists don't believe in idealist archetypes of timeless values. These archetypes of course include truth itself, which is also bound and gagged by conservative statements such as "There is no evolution," or "There is no global warming." This aggravates liberals, especially the scientists among them, many of whom, however, refuse to see the "truth" of the consciousness-resolution of quantum paradoxes, and the "fact" of paranormal phenomena or homeopathic remedies.

The new science bridges the schism. It's dogma-free and inclusive. The data supports it. So what's keeping us from adopting it? A story comes to mind.

During the time of the Italian Renaissance, Duke Federico da Montefeltro was building a palace, but was at a loss as to what to do with the great mass of earth that had been excavated. An abbot is said to have found a solution. Why not dig a hole to dump the excavated earth into? The duke laughed and pointed out that then we'd have to address the problem of the excavated earth from *that* hole. But the abbot did not give up. Make the hole so big that it can hold both, he said.

This abbot would have been quite popular today—witness the kinds of solutions that we often accept in treating some of our most intractable problems. It seems much less daunting to dig a hole or to form an investigative committee than to find a creative solution that may threaten our existing ways of conducting our daily business. However, we can enhance the transition to a dogma-free, polarization-free creative society by thinking creatively. One way to do so would be to inject more creativity into our schools.

Teaching Creativity in Schools

Can society develop such a healthy respect for creativity as to make it pivotal to the education of all its citizens? It certainly can, but here, too, we must loosen our emphasis on doing, on rote learning, and on the three Rs. We need to encourage children to recognize interim failure as an inherent component of creativity, and of eventual success. "Give me a fruitful error any time, full of seeds, bursting with its own correction," said Vilfredo Pareto, the famous 19th-century economist. "You can keep your sterile truths to yourself."

One high school English teacher who understood this point was trying to stimulate her disadvantaged students to read Shakespeare. One day she asked the class about the meaning of a particular passage in *The Taming of the Shrew*. After a long silence, a usually quiet student attempted an answer, but it was wrong. The teacher, however, was so pleased with his unexpected attempt that she reached in her pocket, came up with a dollar bill, and gave it to the student. When another student complained about rewarding a wrong answer, the teacher explained, "Sometimes it takes a lot of wrong answers before you get the right one." Her class later unanimously voted for more Shakespeare.

Education in schools usually proceeds in an unambiguous, linear, and unimaginative fashion. In other words, our scientific culture, with its materialist emphasis, insists too much on prediction and control. As a result imagination and intuition suffer. These aspects of our experience require surrender of control, which permits the radical receptivity of the nonlocal domain. In other words, *being* must accompany *doing* in our schools.

We must never underestimate the role of inspiration, which is born of relaxation, meditation, and communion with nature. Unfortunately, efficiency-minded curricula have little room, if any, for such non-structured activities. When I was a child I was home-schooled until age 11, so I had a lot of time by myself in our backyard, which to my eyes was paradise, full of mango, lychee, jackfruit trees, cranberries, and other lush vegetation. There was also a pond where I skipped stones; I liked watching their ripples extend after they danced over the water. But mostly I reenacted the great epic stories of the *Mahabharata,* which were my secret source of inspiration.

Can we create such opportunities for every schoolchild? We rightly worry about providing breakfast for their physical bodies, but their mental bodies starve from lack of inspiration from the quantum self. Let's face it: Those computer games that many children play so early in their lives may help with concentration, but they are not inspiring. They leave the subtle body untouched except for the lower chakras.

> You've taught your child the three Rs.
> Where would they be if you hadn't?
> But have you remembered the three I's—
> Imagination, intuition, and inspiration?
> Their mastery of the three Rs has cultivated will.
> Without the three I's, how will they learn being?

The Societal Barrier Against Creativity

When we erect a defense against somebody else's creative approach, or contribute to any other inhibition of creativity, we reveal our ignorance. We're acting like the proverbial fool who saws off the branch of the tree that supports him. When an entire society sets up barrier after barrier to creativity, the very foundation of that society becomes shaky; the society becomes moribund.

To put it differently, change happens, like it or not. If we cannot align change to the universal purpose, it will express itself as decay. This is social entropy, and it stinks like gangrene. We need to balance the progress of entropy. Periodically we need to go back to basics and to redefine the very fundamentals on which society is based so that they continue to reflect the particular context in which we live. This redefinition requires creativity.

The United States of America was defined by the U.S. Constitution, by the Bill of Rights, by democracy and capitalism, by liberal education, by individualistic know-how and creative can-do, and by a deep sense of spiritual values. These elements have carried this society through thick and thin. Why? Because during a crisis, whether it's the Civil War or the Great Depression, we have always managed to redefine ourselves. Creativity has always been available, a wellspring of resilience to draw from.

But we cannot take it for granted. In a democracy we elect politicians to represent us and we expect them to take action on our behalf. But early 21st-century politicians, both Democrats and Republicans, are ostriches, up to their necks in the sand of denial. If they remain shackled by dogmatic worldviews that stand in opposition to creativity, it will be difficult to dig ourselves out.

Quantum Activism

Fortunately, the winds of change that are producing both the current crisis and the quantum paradigm shift are strong enough so that only a relatively few dedicated people are needed to take us over the threshold to the next stage of evolution—the primacy of the intuitive mind. If you are reading this book, you may be one of these people, perhaps one of millions all over the world. And you may be ready for what I call quantum activism.

Succinctly put, the goal of quantum activism is to change ourselves and our societies using the transformative principles of quantum physics.[1] Creativity is a major tool of transformation for the quantum activist, so the message of this chapter is this: Join the ranks of those who are harnessing quantum creativity to positive change.

In the myth of the Holy Grail, when Percival comes to the Grail castle where the king is maimed, his first intuition is to ask the king, "What's wrong with you?" But his training as a knight holds him back, and no movement occurs. "Seek, and ye shall find," said Jesus. Ask your question, and the door to creative transformation will open as it did for Percival when he eventually asked his question, and the kingdom was revitalized.

The crippled Grail king is a metaphor for the psyche when the self is dominated by wrong thinking (faulty worldview), wrong living (frantic lifestyle), and wrong livelihood (jobs that leave no room for creativity). Only by continuing to ask the questions that spring from intuition do we make room for creativity, for transformation. As a quantum creative you already engage in right thinking and right living, and hopefully the idea of the economics of consciousness will enable you to achieve a right livelihood. As a quantum activist you will endeavor to bring this sensibility to your fellow humans. The evolutionary movement of consciousness demands it.

Where fear does not create barriers impenetrable
Where the mind is free to take risk,
Where neither reward nor punishment
But honest curiosity motivates,
Where we can listen to the cosmos
Whispering its purposiveness to us,
Into that land of creative freedom
Let my world awake.[2]
—Tagore

PART V

SPIRITUAL CREATIVITY

CHAPTER 18

Inner Creativity: A New Paradigm

People generally practice spirituality under the aegis of a religion. But religions are based on a particular creed; there's not much fervor among them about the nature of reality or God. The word *religion* originated from the Latin *religare,* which means to bind. Spiritual salvation is traditionally based on saving oneself from sin (separateness) and binding oneself with wholeness (God) in heaven. But how many religious people have you met lately who interpret their spiritual search this way?

Different religions say different things. Most speak of spiritual paths as if there were a charted route to follow to achieve your goal. Some religions offer a guru, an enlightened teacher-guide who can take you to the promised land if you just follow. But many find this experience disappointing. What is it missing? With our new science to guide us, it becomes clear. There is no path from an ego driven by base emotions to nonlocal wholeness with its higher values; it takes a quantum leap to get there. And how do we do it? How else but by following our inner creativity?

Making this conceptual shift is a major achievement. And leaps are risky, especially quantum leaps; you don't know where they will take you. Relax. The new science does offer us some guidelines. Ask yourself this: What brought about the urge to try religion or spirituality? Most likely it's dissatisfaction with life's high degree of suffering.

Even if you are a creative person, your accomplishments aren't bringing you much satisfaction. Only by addressing this lack of fulfillment do we make room for inner creativity, for transformation.

Religions and esoteric spiritual traditions leave us frustrated in our pursuit of spirituality by making it an all-or-nothing proposition. God or bust. Kill the ego, the source of your sin and suffering. Surrender to God, or at least to your guru. Humanity has been pursuing these goals for millennia. Look around. Do you see lots of enlightened people?

Rome was not built in a day. And our desires are often conflicting. For example, I may want to search for God, and to work hard to that end; but I also want to enjoy life, to spend time with my friends, and to succeed in my job. These desires are incompatible. The first requires killing the ego; the others require keeping the ego intact. This kind of conflict brings about more suffering, not less.

Now ask yourself, what motivates you to engage in creativity? The unconscious calling you! The archetypes calling you! The universe calling you! So take your quantum leap. Outer accomplishment is no longer enough, but your desire for accomplishment is still there. Bingo! Turn that energy inward and the creative exploration of archetypes yields a new adult ego with a broad positive relationship with the world, increased emotional intelligence, and increased access to the quantum self.

The quantum unconscious pushes us toward our unexplored archetypes. In the movie *Groundhog Day,* the hero is driven to pursue the archetype of love through many incarnations of the same day until he learns love's essence: selflessness. Just like the weatherman played by Bill Murray, we are unconscious of what we are doing when we begin our journey, and we catch on to the game only as we mature.

Embark on the voyage of inner creativity with this goal of embodying the archetypes. Engage in relationships; discover unconditional love. Follow this strategy to emotional intelligence—balancing your negative emotions with positive. Live from your higher values and discover the archetype of goodness. Engage in deep ecology, and teach yourself to be in harmony with your environment. Too much for one lifetime? Of course it is. But this is a quest worthy of many reincarnations.

These creative accomplishments have the side effect of strengthening the ego, which is good, because creative exploration requires a strong ego. This is paradoxical, given that surrendering to God, or the quantum self, requires undermining the ego's narcissism. But there will come a time when your accomplishments, even inner ones, begin to wane in importance. You've been there, done that. This is the time to ease the grip of the ego.

That spirituality ultimately involves a creative change of context in our lives to an indifference to accomplishments is most clearly stated in the story of young Nachiketa in one of the Upanishads. Nachiketa wants to know the spiritual truth, but who can teach it to him? Nobody but Yama, the god of death. So Nachiketa goes to Yama, and for his courage and tenacity Nachiketa is granted enlightenment. This story suggests that the discovery of the spirit, the true nature of nonlocal reality, involves transcending our identity as a conditioned ego: Only the god of death can teach it.

When you set as your goal the embodiment of archetypes, you see that you don't need to be motivated by the negative side of things. Instead of being driven by the need to alleviate suffering, for example, you may find motivation in curiosity. Do you ever wonder what it's like to love unconditionally? Are you curious to find out?

To the extent that we rely on our self-image, we are much like actors. We want to please other people, so we wear masks to meet their expectations. The first stage of developing inner creativity turns out to be shedding the self-image and becoming who we really are—our authentic self. Richard Feynman, the Nobel-winning physicist, wrote a book called *What Do You Care What Other People Think?* We could make this our motto.

Inner Creativity in Acting

In Shakespeare's time, acting was the actor's way of transcending the ego/persona, of arriving at the authentic self/character beyond the masks. The noble heroes of Shakespearian tragedies suffer from inner conflict because of the masks that they wear. There is no resolution except to take off the masks, which is portrayed as the ultimate risk.

Take the case of Hamlet. He is torn between the ego's demand to avenge his father's murder and a higher ethos—thou shalt not kill. The only resolution was tragedy, the loss of the persona, which in his case occurred through actual physical death.

In primitive cultures acting involves wearing masks, through which the wearer becomes the god or animal that he or she is portraying. But anthropologists have noted that masks are worn as catalysts for transformative experience; they are vehicles for inner creativity, for finding the authentic self that lies behind the mask. Masks allow beings to continually transform into other beings. A man is a cougar; a cougar is a bear. The artist is showing that all beings are part of a shared spirit—they are in some way the same.

Today, actors and actresses wear more subtle masks; the characters they portray are usually ordinary people, not gods and animals. But the spiritual purpose of acting remains the same—to discover the unity of the self behind the different masks we all put on. "At one point," muses actor Louis Gossett, Jr., "I don't even know who I am anymore. By the story's end he's [the character] grown into his truest self, and I didn't quite realize what a deep thing that would be to me. When you start to implement yourself and use your soul, you discover more."

Naturally enough, it's far more common for actors and actresses to get caught up in many personas. Instead of exploring the depths of the psyche, they investigate horizontally, expanding the repertoire of masks they are capable of wearing. At this point their performances are no longer contributions to the creative discovery of unity, but exercises in the craft of acting.

These masks are also representations of archetypes, but without any authentic experience of them, we cannot truly live them; they become based on what we think the archetypes are, and thoughts are unreliable. However, the mind does play a powerful—and beneficial— role in this process.

An indispensable practice for union with the authentic self is self-observation, a radical, unflinchingly honest, nonjudgmental observation of your playacting behavior with others. This exploration of your specific rationalizations, justifications, and other defenses is coupled with inquiry into your inner motivations, feelings, and thoughts while you are doing it. With ongoing awareness you can penetrate the deeper and subtler layers of your persona, a process that is by turns profoundly illuminating and acutely painful. When you engage in this practice with compassion for yourself, your capacity for compassion will deepen and extend to others.

Creative Exploration of Love

In the 2012 presidential campaign, a conservative candidate laid out the doctrine that sex must be used for reproductive purposes only. In contrast, liberals tend to see sex as a form of pleasure. The evolution of consciousness demands more of us than these two primitive views of sexuality.

Because of our brain structure, our sexuality is aroused easily and often by a variety of stimuli. When we are teenagers and these feelings are unfamiliar we can become confused about our sexuality and the nature of love. Some religions address this problem by advocating celibacy before marriage, but unfortunately this is often done without much guidance as to why or how. The original idea could have been good: Remain celibate until you discover romantic love, which can be the beginning of a creative journey toward unconditional, archetypal love. But in its current limited form, this spiritual admonition will do little to dissipate teen confusion.

If a teenager has sex without understanding its creative potential, he or she will blindly respond to the brain's biological imperative. Since the fulfillment of sexual pleasure with a partner raises vital energy to the third chakra, associated with the ego identity, personal power enters the equation. Hence it becomes common to think of "sexual conquests" in a way that is disconnected from romantic love.

In the Western world, this experience of sex as power develops early, especially in men. What happens when we eventually discover a partner with whom our heart chakra resonates? We enter the relationship, but we tend not to give up the habit of conquest. So when romance wanes, which it does sooner or later because we habituate to every new experience, sex-as-power moves into the ascendancy. We then have a choice. We can look for another romantic partner, or go deeper into the existing relationship to explore its creative potential.

From the perspective of quantum consciousness, to enter into marriage is to change the equation of sex: I commit to changing my pattern of using sex for power to using sex to make love. This requires allowing energy to rise to the heart after a sexual encounter, which means letting ourselves become vulnerable. Marriage is a commitment to make love, not war.

Unfortunately, this agreement has to find its counterpart in the subtle bodies of the partners as well. Here, too, individual ego conditioning runs deep; territoriality and competitiveness can bring the energy down from the heart chakra to the navel chakra, prompting a return to narcissism. When his wife expressed dissatisfaction with their marriage, the husband said, "I don't get it. Your job is to make me happy, and I am. So what's the problem?"

A *Calvin and Hobbes* cartoon adds to this portrayal of narcissism. Calvin says, "I am at peace with the world. I'm completely serene." When pressed by Hobbes, he clarifies, "*I* am here so everybody can do what *I* want." (My italics.) From this place love is an act of magnanimity, proffered from a superior position in a hierarchical relationship. But this is not love; instead of leading to connection, it leads to isolation.

When we become aware of our loneliness, we begin to inquire why we are lonely, why we do not feel loved, and why, in truth, we cannot give unselfish love either. We become curious: If we give unconditional love, does the emptiness fill? We stoke the fire of curiosity until this becomes a burning question. It is then that we have become serious about engaging the creative process of discovering love. The next step is unconscious processing.

Unconscious Processing in the Exploration of Love

Consider the double-slit setup in which a beam of electrons passes through a double-slit screen before hitting a second fluorescent screen. After passing through the first screen, the possibility wave of each electron divides into two waves that "interfere" with one another; the result is displayed as spots on the fluorescent screen. If the crests of the two waves arrive together at a place on the screen, we get constructive interference (reinforcement of possibility [figure 22B])—the probability for an electron to arrive is maximum—that shows as bright spots on the screen. Crest and trough arriving together at a place make destructive interference—no possibility of any electron landing there at all (figure 22C)—and show as dark regions on the fluorescent screen. The total pattern, called an interference pattern, consists of these alternate bright and dark regions (figure 22D).

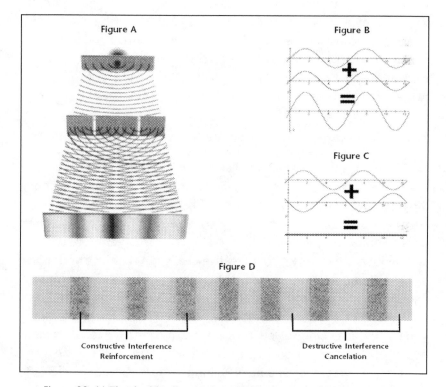

Figure 22: (a) The double-slit experiment with electrons. (b) Waves arriving at the fluorescent screen in phase reinforce each other (constructive interference). (c) Waves arriving at a point out of phase cancel each other out. (d) The resulting interference pattern of alternate bright and dark fringes.

What does all this have to do with creativity in relationships? Our conditioning does not allow incoming stimuli to evoke the full range of possible responses. Instead it narrows the choices so we respond with the perspective of our ego. This is like the case of the electron passing through a single slit before striking the fluorescent screen. If we pass the electron through a double slit, the possibility pool is enhanced enormously. Unconscious processing always precedes a creative insight. The more we can generate quantum waves of possibility in our unconscious mind, the more effective our unconscious processing will be.

Having a committed intimate relationship is like having a double slit for all your incoming stimuli. The truth is, you may not yet consciously recognize your partner's various contexts for seeing things, but your unconscious is already considering them. Your possibility pool to choose from is now that much bigger. With this dynamic in place, sooner or later you will fall into a creative awareness of "otherness of the other" (to use sociologist Carol Gilligan's language).

Inviting Quantum Consciousness to Resolve Your Conflicts

Now that a truly respectful relationship is under way, you can take more risks. In the movie *The Wedding Date,* to my great satisfaction, the hero said to the heroine that he'd like to marry her because he'd rather fight with her than make love with another person. To practice unconditional love, it's important to also recognize your love partner as "the intimate enemy." Your creative challenge is to love your partner in spite of your differences. And when these differences cause a fight, so be it. Remain there until a quantum leap takes place, or until the situation become unbearable at your present stage of emotional development. Unresolved conflicts are guaranteed to bring new possibilities into your pool of experience for unconscious processing. Gradually we become capable of waiting out unresolved conflicts indefinitely: Now not only are you present as individuals, you are also now an "us."

This practice of holding unresolved conflicts until resolution comes from higher consciousness is difficult, but the rewards are enormous. The conditions you impose on your love fall away. Once we can love unconditionally, needs give way to choices. We're no longer helpless in the face of sexual desire. Now the whole world can become the object of our passionate love.

On special nights when the moon is full, legend has it that Krishna dances with his ten thousand consorts all at once. Such is the power of Krishna's unconditional love that it exceeds the limits of space and time. This is quantum love.

The Awakening of Supramental Intelligence

In our journey of transformation we have to explore each of the major archetypes. The primary objective is to move beyond rational intelligence, which does not bring us happiness. The creative exploration of unconditional love helps us develop emotional intelligence, and with it the ability to maintain intimate relationships.

Each of us has to discover creatively the truth of "Love your neighbor." Only through a direct quantum leap (an insight) can you experience oneness with your neighbor, and really live this truth with effortless consistency. Being good to your neighbor then becomes an ongoing renewal of relationship—grounded not in rote repetition but in present-centered, creative fluidity. You have discovered ethical living.

Etymologically, "eco" comes from the Greek word *oikos* (meaning place) and "logy" from the Greek *logos* (meaning knowledge). So ecology is about knowledge of the place in which we live. But we live not only in our external environment, but also in our internal. Deep ecology, a concept developed by ecologist Arne Næss, appeals to us to take ethical responsibility for both our gross and subtle worlds.

As our archetypal accomplishments accumulate, the ego-identity shifts to a more balanced relationship with the quantum self. I call this the awakening of supramental intelligence, called *buddhi* in Sanskrit. Etymologically, intelligence comes from the root word *intelligo*, which means, "to select among." Indeed, with the awakening of supramental intelligence, we become aware that we are selecting from among all the possibilities available, not just within a limited range. Now we begin to take responsibility for our choices.

Supramental intelligence brings a welcome freedom from compulsive self-preoccupation. You may sometimes feel this freedom when you sing in the shower or walk in the woods, but can you imagine it during what you call chores, what you call boredom, or even what you call suffering? It is like dancing through life. "Will you, won't you, will you, won't you, won't you join the dance?" This exuberant invitation from Lewis Carroll is always open to all of us, and when supramental intelligence awakens, we accept it.

Carl Jung put considerable emphasis on inner creativity, which he said leads to "individuation"—a stage of development in which the person's individuality is firmly established within a cosmic unity.

> [Archetypal] Journeys bring power and love
> Back into you. If you can't go somewhere,
> Move in the passageways of the self.
> They are like shafts of light,
> Always changing, and you change
> When you explore them.[1]
> —Rumi

CHAPTER 19

Self-Realization

Why are so many people these days taking pills for anxiety and depression? Separation from wholeness, which is on the rise in modern society, is experienced as suffering. Some of us shove the suffering under the rug and seek pleasure as a way to find relief. Others turn to creativity. The accomplishments of creative intelligence bring us satisfaction. But subtle suffering in the form of boredom remains. It's because we're experiencing the deep unease that the Buddha called *dukkha*. This is the realization of Buddha's first noble truth—life is suffering. Suffering now comes from the duality of living with two identities—the ego and the quantum self.

When one is bored even with the creative accomplishments of knowing and living the archetypes—been there, done that—the creative person's curiosity becomes intense, leading to a burning question: Can I go beyond all duality? The state of "no ego-self" is true self-realization; therein lies the spiritual joy that Hindus call *ananda*. Can I shift my identity to the quantum self and forever enjoy the bliss of that union? This leads to the intense desire to know the nature of consciousness itself. This fuels new inquiry. Who am I? What is my true nature? Where is it rooted?

There is a lasting myth in some spiritual traditions that to be truly initiated into self-realization you must have a guru, an enlightened teacher. But the quantum self, the divine spirit, is the only guru you will ever need. If you are sinking in quicksand you cannot pull yourself up by your own bootstraps, but it is possible to bootstrap yourself out of the trap of ego-identity. This is because although some ego functions are necessary to sustain life, an ego-identity is not.

Using inner creativity you lift yourself beyond the simple hierarchy of the ego-identity to the tangled hierarchy of the quantum self. You cannot reach that goal through a process that demands a simple hierarchy, like some power-based guru-disciple relationships. If you encounter one of those rare individuals who understands and relates through tangled-hierarchical relationships, that's different. In India, such a teacher is called a *sadguru.*

Now comes the quintessential question. How are the stages of inner creativity that catapult us into the exalted realm of the quantum self different from the usual stages of creativity? To answer this question, let's begin by looking at the first step.

Initial Preparation

Traditionally, Eastern preparation for the spiritual journey of inner creativity involved the study of the literature in order to achieve an intellectual understanding of the philosophy of consciousness presented by philosophers and mystics through the ages. If you were part of a religious lineage, you studied the scriptures to understand the meaning behind the form of particular rituals and practices.

You would also find a guru (although not necessarily a human guru), to whom you would surrender your ego. It took many years of study, rituals, and meditation (much like the creative process) to break through to the realization that "I am the innermost self." In Hinduism this union was the culmination of wisdom, the *gyana yoga* (in Sanskrit) path to self-realization. But this wisdom did not help much with living in relationship with the world. You would know the truth, but you still would not know how to live it. So after the dawning of wisdom, you went on to practice love (*bhakti yoga* in Sanskrit). Traditions such as Christianity and Sufism tried to reverse the process, putting love before wisdom. But this did not work well either, because without wisdom it is very difficult to master the faith in quantum consciousness required to take the journey of self-realization.

Today, as the science of self-realization is becoming clear, we have discovered a new gyana yoga, Western-style. First we acquire wisdom through the theoretical resolution of quantum paradoxes; next we reassure ourselves that the important elements of the theory, such as nonlocality and downward causation, are experimentally verified. In this way we gain faith in this new science. This is part of our preparation. This is, in Buddha's terminology, right thinking.

At the next stage of preparation, we investigate the archetypes. This takes many lifetimes; if you already have achieved detachment from accomplishments (called *vairagya* in Sanskrit), and love, ethics, deep ecology, and emotional intelligence come easily for you, then you know you are ready for the final journey of self-realization. You know already how to live your right thinking. In Buddha's terminology, this is called right living.

If some aspect of right living is still lacking, take it on. Otherwise, the need for accomplishment will still be there after you experience self-realization, and this will block some important manifestations to come. Some self-proclaimed gurus enjoy the pleasures of the ego, causing much confusion. It does not mean that they are not self-realized, but it does mean that they have not been able to take upon themselves the task of fully manifesting the quantum self-identity from which only virtuous action would flow.

The final preparation for the journey of self-realization is to find your right livelihood, which you must not use for accomplishments that lead to ego building.

Alternate Work and Incubation: Will and Surrender

Much of the work of self-exploration is unconscious. During the stage of unconscious processing we refrain from actively pursuing the problem at hand. In the inner creativity of self-realization we become quiet, silencing the voice of the accomplisher. We surrender to the flow of life rather than trying to push the river this way or that.

Moudgalyana came to Buddha with many questions he had asked of all the teachers he had encountered. But Buddha responded by asking, "Do you want to know the answers or the questions?"

Startled, Moudgalyana did not know what to say. Buddha elaborated, "All worthwhile answers have to grow inside you. What I say is irrelevant. So stay with me in silence for a year. After the year, if you still want to ask, I will answer." Moudgalyana did so, and after the year came to an end, when Buddha asked him if he had any questions, he said nothing. Now he understood the importance of silence for self-realization.

Supplementing unconscious processing with conscious striving is often advantageous. Some people are so entrenched in their egos that a great deal of practice is needed before they're able to abandon their dug-in positions. Others find it easy. In one Zen story a spiritual seeker meets an extraordinary spiritual family in which all members have awakened to their Buddha nature. In answer to the seeker's question, "Is it difficult to awaken to our true nature?" the father says, "It is very, very difficult." The mother says, "It's the easiest thing in the world." The son says, "It's neither." Finally the daughter says, "If you make it difficult, it is. If you don't, it's not."

The Role of Encounter in the Inner Creativity of Self-Realization

As I mentioned earlier, the inner creativity of self-realization involves achieving a resolution between our ego and our quantum modalities. The existentialist philosopher Martin Buber has called this the I-thou encounter; it's even more intense than creativity in service of accomplishments because your purpose now is transformation of your identity, a radical change to your adult ego. Radical change requires radical intensity.

A young man did not see how it was possible to concentrate on a mantra even for a few minutes. So his teacher, who happened to be the king, ordered the young man to carry a vessel full of oil three times around the palace. "And while you carry the oil," cautioned the king, "be careful that not a single drop falls to the ground. A swordsman will follow you, and he will cut off your head if any of the oil spills." As he carried out the King's command, the young man discovered the art of successful concentration.

Physician and spiritual teacher Richard Moss found that impending surgery also fostered the meditative intensity I've been discussing; the healing path can be very helpful for self-realization. When the mystic/psychologist Richard Alpert (also known as Ram Dass) worked on a prison project, he was impressed with the level of awareness of the inmates on death row. Hospice workers also find that high levels of intensity become available to people facing death. But extreme circumstances are not a requirement. The basis of the teachings of Krishnamurti was simple curiosity. Just observe; just look.

Ultimately, we are afraid of intense practice. It's like the story of the chicken and the pig traveling together. They saw a diner with a sign advertising a bacon-and-egg special, and the hungry chicken wanted to stop there. But the pig balked, protesting, "You have to make only a contribution. But for me, that's total commitment." The mystic Ligia Dantes suggests watching our fear and learning to discriminate between fear as a natural survival instinct and fear as the need to perpetuate the illusions of the ego-identity. When you shed fantasy you can more readily invite intensity into your practice.

"If I give up my ego, what's left?" This is the question—formed entirely from our desires, fears, attachments, etc.—that makes us shy away from honest self-scrutiny and from surrendering to the quantum self. Is there life after shifting your center of being beyond the ego? You have to ask the question with intensity, to take a risk with no surety of reward, and to accept the anguish of waiting for your new life to spring forth.

> The travail of the night
> Will it not usher the dawn?
> In the night of sorrow, under death's blow,
> When man bursts his mortal bounds,
> Will not God stand revealed
> In His glory?
> —Tagore

Big Insight

The mystic Franklin Merrell-Wolff, a trained mathematician and philosopher, practiced the path of wisdom for years with great intensity. Then two things happened. He came across the wisdom of the Indian mystic Shankara through his book, *Crest Jewel of Discrimination.* Distilled to its essence, Shankara's insight was this: Atman (the quantum self) is Brahman (consciousness, the foundation of being). Merrell-Wolff began to tirelessly ponder this wisdom. Then one day he realized that there was nothing to seek. To his amazement, this realization was followed by an experience of the quantum self.

What actually takes place in this direct encounter with the quantum self? Merrell-Wolff is quite specific:

> The first discernible effect on consciousness was something that I may call *a shift in the base of consciousness.* . . . I knew myself to be beyond *space, time, and causality.* . . . Closely associated with the foregoing realization there is a feeling of *complete freedom.* . . . I did not attempt to stop the activity of the mind, but simply very largely ignored the stream of thought. . . . The result was that I was in a sort of compound state wherein I was both here and "There," with the objective consciousness less acute than normal.[2]

In the moment of spiritual illumination, quantum self-awareness floods the field of attention; secondary-awareness processes (related to memory and ego) continue, but are given no attention or importance. Some people declare that they are "enlightened" as a result of the experience of self-realization. But there is a fallacy here. As Lao Tzu used to say, "The one who knows cannot say, the one who says cannot know." So here is a genuine difference between inner creativity of accomplishments and the inner creativity of self-realization. In the former, the ego is the central player. This is appropriate, and does no harm. But in inner creativity of self-realization, any such involvement of the ego is a detriment to the process.

Ram Dass went public with his enlightenment, only to realize years later how the declaration had interfered with the transformation of his being. After he corrected his mistake, his spiritual flowering resumed. In other words, humility is a necessary ingredient of self-realization. Humility is the recognition that a transpersonal consciousness beyond ego, beyond even the quantum self, is potentially in charge.

What brings you to the path of self-realization,
Oh traveler? Do you seek to know yourself?
Have you exhausted your accomplishments?
Have you manifested the archetypes in your living?

Meditate hard, practice silence—until,
Your striving exhausted, you surrender
In utter humility.
Then, enfolded in your experience
Of oneness with the universe,
Do you think you are enlightened?
Is this your new identity?

CHAPTER 20

What Is Enlightenment?

During the earlier stages of the process of inner creativity lead-ing to self-realization, a moving away from the world, a renunciation, takes place. During manifestation, there is a reentry into the world, but from no fixed center of self-identity, for this has shifted beyond ego. This reentry problem is alluded to in the Zen saying "Before awak-ening, mountains are mountains and lakes are lakes. Then mountains are not mountains, lakes are not lakes. After awakening mountains are mountains, lakes are lakes."

With the realization of a deeper self, our identification with the ego increasingly gives way to the quantum self, and we try to mani-fest this in our daily living. To describe this phenomenon, East Indian mystic Ramakrishna used the analogy of a salt figurine dipped into the ocean. The figurine dissolves; its saltiness remains, but its separate structure and identity no longer exist. This is the goal of the creative act of self-realization. The challenge is to remain aware of the move-ments of consciousness as they manifest reality.

All three great East Indian mystics of recent times, Ramakrishna, Ramana Maharshi, and Sri Aurobindo, spent long years in silence after their insight of self-realization. The sixth patriarch of Chan Buddhism, Huineng, was a humble cook for 12 years after his enlightenment be-fore circumstances catapulted him to public life. As the center of the self shifts beyond ego, action increasingly comes from the quantum self, from primary awareness. At the cremation grounds in India, an attendant stands by the burning pyre with a stick to see that no part of the body escapes. When the job is done, the attendant throws the stick on the pyre. This is the destination.

Savikalpa and Nirvikalpa Samadhi

In self-realization, the subject, the object, and the entire field of awareness all tend to become one. In yoga literature this is called *savikalpa samadhi;* in Sanskrit *samadhi* means the balance between the two poles of subject and object. *Savikalpa* means "with separation." In other words, in this experience we become aware of the dependent co-arising of the universal quantum self and the world, albeit with some sense of separation. We never *experience* consciousness as *un*divided from its possibilities. In other words, savikalpa samadhi is as deep as experience can go. Now we see clearly that we are at one with the (unconscious) creative forces of the universe.

Very confusingly to the ordinary mind, Eastern literature refers to another kind of samadhi called *nirvikalpa samadhi.* The Sanskrit word *nirvikalpa* means "without split"—without subject-object separation. But we know from quantum mechanics that any experience involves the collapse of possibility into actuality. If there is no experience without a subject-object split, what does this represent?

To understand, consider deep sleep. In deep sleep there is no subject-object split and there is no experience. Yet this is an accepted state of consciousness. So nirvikalpa samadhi can be understood as a deeper sleep in which some special unconscious processing takes place, much like the "experience" of a near-death survivor who sees himself from a distance and remembers this on being revived. Since experience is impossible when you are dead, the near-death survivor's memory upon being revived has to be recognized to be the result of "delayed choice," explained earlier. Similarly, knowledge arises in the mind of the yogi in nirvikalpa samadhi upon waking up. This knowledge is what the East Indian sage Patanjali meant when he said, "Meditate on knowledge that comes during sleep." Some people call this kind of knowledge the result of *imperience,* not experience.

What is the special vision that is revealed upon waking up from nirvikalpa? The mystic sage Swami Sivananda describes it this way:

> There are two kinds of . . . nirvikalpa samadhi. In the first the jnani [wise person], by resting in Brahman [Sanskrit word for Godhead], sees [processes] the whole world within himself as a movement of ideas, as a mode of being or a mode of his own existence. . . . This is the highest state of realization . . .
>
> In the second variety the world vanishes from view and the jnani rests on pure attributeless Brahman.[1]

Clearly the first kind of nirvikalpa samadhi is the ultimate state of unconscious processing, in which we process the entire world of quantum possibilities, including the archetypes. Sivananda's second nirvikalpa state is called *turiya*. Turiya is a deeper state of non-experience, or imperience. Can any form of consciousness be deeper than the unconscious processor of quantum possibilities of the whole universe? What came before that? Consciousness with all possibilities, no limitations imposed, not even quantum laws. When all possibilities are included, there is no quality, and there is nothing to process, which is the reason Buddhists call this state of consciousness the Great Void; Hindus call it *nirguna,* or attributeless; and Christians call it Godhead (prior to God).

The spiritual literature of India claims that people with nirvikalpa capacity are totally transformed, that their identity completely shifts to the quantum self except when the ego is needed for everyday chores, for ego-functions. So when it comes to enlightenment, self-realization is not the end of the road. You have to manifest the quantum self in everyday living. A vestige of ego-identity remains.

The situation is drastically different for a person who has realized turiya. Now there is no longer any "thing" to manifest. This is *nirvana,* to use the language of Buddha—the state of no desire. When this state becomes effortless, there is nothing more to be accomplished, there is no need to take rebirth. So if liberation means freedom from a birth-death-rebirth cycle, then liberation arrives with nirvana. But if you have the exalted notion that liberation means total freedom, forget it. As long as we live in this body we cannot be totally free of ego conditioning; we cannot always reside in the quantum self. Hence the wise koan, How does a Zen master go to the bathroom? The same way everyone else does.

So in esoteric Hinduism there is the concept of liberation in the body that then is recognized to have some limitations. Only in death do we find total freedom.

The end of Buddha's journey is nirvana—cessation of all desires.
When all your identity structures give way to a profound fluidity,
Only then is there unending celebration.
Call it enlightenment if you like.
This bloom has no name, only fragrance.

PART VI

BRINGING CREATIVITY TO THE CENTER OF YOUR LIFE

CHAPTER 21

Practice, Practice, Practice

In the familiar anecdote, a pedestrian in a busy street of midtown Manhattan asks another pedestrian, "How do I get to Carnegie Hall?" The man he asks happens to be a musician, so instead of replying with directions to the famous music venue he says, "Practice, practice, practice."

The same holds true for finding the way to creativity. When novelist Natalie Goldberg suffered from writer's block, her Zen master told her, "Make writing your practice." After all the dedication to process, there is still that question of practice.

Both inner and outer creativity are about freedom. Engaging in inner creativity is the way to access greater and greater freedom by cleaning up your inner being; outer creativity should become the expression of your inner freedom in the outer world. Carl Rogers said creativity requires keeping an open mind. Can you practice keeping your mind open?

The problem here is the paradoxical role that ego plays. You cannot be creative without a strong ego to manage the uncertainty that comes with any creative endeavor. Creativity also requires that you continually take the risk of changing the character of the ego. You become afraid: What if changing my ego affects the very strength that makes me creative?

Until now—with a few exceptions like William Blake, Walt Whitman, Rabindranath Tagore, and Carl Jung—inner creativity has been used primarily to achieve spiritual liberation from the world. But spirituality does not have to be world-negating. If, as we discussed earlier, the world is evolving spiritually, why not become attuned to that movement of consciousness?

Let's consider seven practices that can help you break through the patterns of ego to allow more participation in your life by quantum consciousness. You can think of these practices as a purification of your creative sattva. You can also think of them as vehicles for awakening your supramental intelligence—a more integrated mode of being and identity from which to create, and from which to fulfill your human potential. The practices are:

1. Intention-setting
2. Slowing down—allowing openness, awareness, and sensitivity
3. Concentration, or focusing
4. Do-be-do-be-do—alternating action and relaxed incubation
5. Imagination and dreaming
6. Working with Jungian archetypes and creating positive emotional brain circuits
7. Remembering your dharma

The Practice of Intention-Setting

The truth is, our mind is comfortable, although not always happy, to reside in the cocoon of the ego. Intention-setting is our way out. Remember, we can set an intention with our ego, but what actually happens depends entirely on our degree of attunement with quantum consciousness. The following practice is set up accordingly.

Sit comfortably. Engage in a body-awareness exercise to banish tension. Become aware of your toes, and breathe into them so they relax. Do the same for the tops of the feet, then the undersides of your feet, and the ankles, moving up your legs, torso, arms, neck, and head. Repeat this process with any part of the body still in need of release. Now that you're relaxed, remember that an intention must start with the ego, so use your will to manifest it.

Now, at the second stage, recognize that you can have what you intend in two ways: You can have it all for yourself, or in such a way that everyone (including you) enjoys the fruit of your intention. Choose the latter, expanding your intention to include everyone in your immediate vicinity; then let your attention extend outward like a ripple in a pond, including everyone in your town or city, in your county, in your state, in your country, on this planet, and finally in the whole universe.

In the third stage let your intention gradually become a prayer: *If my intention resonates with the movement of the whole, then let it come to fruition.*

In the fourth stage, allow the prayerful mind to become silent, meditative. Stay in silent meditation for a few minutes.

Use this practice whenever you wish to support an intention with all your creative power.

The Practices for Slowing Down: Open Mind, Awareness, and Sensitivity

Underneath all creativity lies a paradox. How can we know so much and yet not know? A professor went to a Zen master to learn about Zen. The master offered the professor some tea. As the master was making the tea, the professor began to show off his erudition, expounding on his knowledge of Zen. When the tea was made, the master began pouring the tea into the professor's cup. He went on pouring even after the cup was full, spilling the tea onto the table and the floor until the professor cried, "Stop! My cup is full." The Zen master said, "So is your mind. How can I teach you if your mind is so full of your own ideas?"

A creative mind never fully identifies with what's in it. A creative mind retains a certain amount of naiveté, always ready to ask the basic questions. Nobody told a supposedly not-so-bright boy named Albert Einstein that aspiring researchers of physics are not supposed to ask basic questions; so the child approached questions about light, space, and time with "beginner's mind," and eventually discovered relativity.

But the situation is more complicated for an educated adult who has to learn a lot of other people's opinions about a lot of things. This person has to remain open to new possibilities and yet have a large repertoire of knowledge to draw upon. How does one have both mastery and beginner's mind?

Buddhists and Jains in India sometimes debate about what it means to know everything, to be omniscient. The Jains tell a story of two artists competing for the king's favor. One artist has filled one wall of the art gallery, and the king is very pleased. "How can you beat this?" the king asks the second artist. "I can't. So I have painted exactly the same thing," replies the artist, opening the drapes on the opposite wall, and the king is amazed. Indeed, the same painting shows up in dazzling beauty, replicating the original piece of art in every intricate detail. And why not? The second wall is a mirror. So, say the Jains, be like the mirror and reflect perfectly all knowledge. That is omniscience.

But Buddhists see it differently. Why be burdened with all your knowledge when you don't need it all the time? Let knowledge come to you as required. In this way of thinking the creative person develops mastery, but does not dwell on the information gained. If, after mastery is attained, we want to keep it available for instant recall, we have to practice retrieving it, and in the process we come to identify with it. In this way we develop a Jain fast mind, always thinking. But if we practice in such a way as to give up speed, we won't identify with our reservoir of knowledge. But how do you practice this slowness of mind?

In some spiritual traditions like Zen, a slow mind is also called, somewhat confusingly, an empty mind. Can our mind's space be really empty? Of course not. Memories are always generating thoughts. But a slow mind does not identify with the thoughts, it does not own them; in that sense it is empty—empty of ownership.

The meditative practice for cultivating beginner's mind, or emptiness of mind, is called awareness meditation. As thoughts arise in your awareness, you watch them parade like clouds floating by in a tranquil sky, without attachment or interference. If and when you recognize that you are paying too much attention to a particular thought, bring your awareness firmly back to dispassionate witnessing. Practice this choiceless awareness 15 or 20 minutes a day; don't overdo it, at least at the beginning.

Since awareness doesn't take place in isolation, but always comes in conjunction with the physical and subtle body, it helps to slow down the physical organs and also their correlated energy fields. You can practice a slow version of hatha yoga or stretching techniques for the former, and breathing practices like pranayama for the latter. There are also martial arts techniques such as tai chi and aikido for slowing down the movement of vital energy.

The Practice of Concentration

Awareness meditation is good for teaching us how to be, but that is only half of what is required for creative insight. Do we just combine slow mind with fast mind to get to do-be-do-be-do? No, it is subtler than that. Being hyperactive, the fast mind is unable to concentrate. By contrast, the doing mind of creativity is a focused mind. Two-time Nobel Prize winner Marie Curie had such powers of concentration that once her siblings made a wall of tables and chairs around her while she was working at her desk. Marie was oblivious to what was going on until she got up and the furniture crashed around her, to her huge embarrassment.

There is a similar story about Indian physicist Meghnad Saha, who, while working on a problem in astrophysics as he walked, encountered a boy and conversed with him. Upon returning home he told his wife about this pleasant interaction, whereupon his wife patiently reminded him that the boy was his own son. One morning Albert Einstein told his wife, "Darling, I've got a wonderful idea," and disappeared into his study, not to reemerge for weeks. Sir Isaac

Newton's sister used to complain that when he was busy with his research, Sir Isaac often forgot to eat.

Similar stories abound for creative people. Where do they get such powers of concentration? More to the point, can you and I cultivate this ability? And finally, why is concentration so important to creativity?

Cognitive research confirms that we humans are serial processors at the conscious level. The brain is very, very fast, but our consciousness only manages one discrete thought at a time. Not only does this mean that whatever you're thinking at a given moment is eclipsing all other thoughts, but that consciously repeating the thought has the same effect. This is how a burning question maintains itself at the forefront of your mind. This is where creative people have an edge with their intense curiosity. However, in times of crisis we all go into survival mode, which trumps everything else, and we all can easily find burning questions.

A technique called concentration meditation provides something akin to a creative person's pressing question. Known by its Sanskrit name, *japa,* in one Hindu version of concentration meditation you choose a short word (a monosyllabic mantra such as the Sanskrit *om* works well) and repeat the word internally. When other thoughts interfere—as they will, especially in the beginning—and you become aware of them, firmly bring your attention back to your Sanskrit word. Concentration meditation in aid of creativity is best served by regular practice for a short period (15 or 20 minutes are adequate) every day, supplemented by an effort to bring the practice into life situations as appropriate.

To be creative, you must distinguish between desire and will. They are related, but desire puts us on a treadmill to nowhere, whereas will in the service of creativity has the full support of the universe. When you want to lose weight but also want to eat sweets, you're struggling with desire; conflict always accompanies desire. In contrast, when you really commit to something, desire gives way to will, which has the power to say no to conditioning. This is where concentration meditation can help. Look at Vincent van Gogh—it was will that guided him to paint *Sunflowers* in the blazing summer sun of southern France; no mere desire to do so would have sufficed.

Whereas japa and mantras focus on the auditory sense and work very well for some people to focus concentration, for others visualization comes more easily. If you fall into this latter category, try visualizing anything that engages your interest: a flower, the face of a loved one, or an archetypal symbol like a mandala. Initially the image will be fuzzy or fragmentary, but with practice it will stabilize to such an extent that you can evoke it at will, and even manipulate it.

There is a brain aspect of concentration that neuroscientists working with creative people have uncovered. Ordinarily the brain's right temporoparietal junction (r-TPJ) is always reading stimuli, trying to sort out what is relevant and what is not. We can concentrate fully by learning how to block out this area of the brain, turning off all distraction or sideways wandering. Jazz musicians for whom improvisation is essential block out their r-TPJ, says the Johns Hopkins researcher Charles Limb. Researchers are likely to find the same effect at work in concentration meditation.

Concentration can lead you to such states of absorption that the object is no longer independent from consciousness. As virtuoso pianist Lorin Hollander said about his childhood piano practice, "When I played a note I would become that note." It is in the spontaneity of these states of quantum modality that creative ideas, insights, understandings, and visions crystallize. Novelist Gustave Flaubert said, "When I wrote about Emma Bovary's poisoning [in *Madame Bovary*] I had the taste of arsenic so strongly in my mouth, I was so thoroughly poisoned myself, that I gave myself two bouts of indigestion, one after another, two very real bouts since I vomited up my entire dinner."

The Practice of Do-Be-Do-Be-Do

There are many cases of concentration meditation culminating in the state of consciousness called *samadhi,* which Abraham Maslow called a peak experience. This is the state in which one recognizes the world in its true nature—neither external objects nor one's self seem separate from consciousness. Many years ago I practiced japa for seven days and had such an experience. On the face of it, japa is just concentration on a mantra. But sages say that after a while the japa become internalized. What does that mean? It continues to take place in the unconscious while you are consciously attending to your chores. Do-be-do-be-do!

I described my experience this way:

> On a sunny November morning, I was sitting quietly in my chair in my office doing japa. This was the seventh day since I had started, and I still had a lot of energy left. About an hour of japa, and I got an urge to take a walk outside. I continued my mantra deliberately as I walked out of my office, then out of the building, across the street, and onto the grassy meadow. And then the universe opened up to me.

> I seemed to be one with the cosmos, the grass, the trees, the sky. Sensations were present, in fact, intensified beyond belief. But these sensations were pale in significance compared to the feeling of love that followed, a love that engulfed everything in my consciousness—until I lost comprehension of the process. This was *ananda,* bliss.

> There was a moment or two of which I don't have any description, no thoughts, not even feeling. Afterwards, it was just bliss. It was still bliss as I walked back to my office. It was bliss when I talked to our cantankerous secretary, but she was beautiful in the bliss, and I loved her. It was bliss when I taught my large freshman class; the noise in the back rows, even the back-row kid who threw a paper airplane was bliss.

> It was all bliss.

To be creative, says philosopher Erich Fromm, one "has to give up holding onto himself as a thing and begin to experience himself only in the process of creative response; paradoxically enough, if he can experience himself in this process, he loses himself. He transcends the boundaries of his own person, and at the very moment when he feels 'I am,' he also feels 'I am you,' 'I am one with the whole world.'"

The process Fromm is referring to is, of course, do-be-do-be-do, alternating focused doing with relaxed being leading to samadhi. My japa practice did begin through an act of will, but I noticed that after a time the japa must have been going on in the unconscious while I was carrying out my daily activities, because whenever I looked for it I found it.

People often ask me if I practice currently. The answer is yes. It is a practice in which I try to be aware while doing ordinary tasks. It's not unlike awareness meditation, but I also occasionally check the energy in my heart chakra, visualizing it connected to all other people's heart chakras by a golden thread. The idea is to engage in everything I do with an open heart.

Christian contemplatives practice while holding the image of Jesus in their hearts. Brother Lawrence spent his life "practicing the presence of God," which transformed him. In Dzogchen, Tibetan meditators practice "presence." I suppose you can call what I do "practicing the presence of love."

The Practice of Imagination and Dreaming

When we perceive something out in the world, an external stimulus produces a brain image for which we find a correlated mental state, thereby giving it meaning. When we use our imagination we start with a mental state and find a match for it in language or visual representations in the brain's repertoire; we see a visual image even though there is no external object. Every once in a while we fall into intuitive states of primary awareness, unleashing images or thoughts we've never considered before. Now, using the brain's neuroplasticity, we can make new maps of mental states. As a pundit once said, "Genius is the capacity to treat objects of the imagination as real, and even to manipulate them as such."

Now you can understand what Coleridge meant when he distinguished between fancy and imagination. Fancy is just a frivolous expression of the intellect, the playful doodling of the ego. But imagination, said Coleridge, springs "from elemental parts of the spirit shared by all." In our ego mode, we make known images from our past experience. But when we elude the ego, as we do in a dream state, we may more easily fall into primary awareness of the quantum self. Then we can explore truly creative imagery, and manifest the unknown.

When we dream, the otherwise vigilant ego relaxes, allowing us to dip into the unknown in ways that the conscious mind rarely permits. In dreams, the unconscious becomes the major player. One of the major ideas of this book, the importance of do-be-do-be-do in the creative process, came to me in a dream. I was observing a group of very active abstract figures, who were dancing, gamboling, and frolicking about. A voice in the background introduced them as the angels of doing. But soon these figures were replaced by other abstract figures—quieter, more relaxed ones. The voice proclaimed them angels of being. But then the angels of doing came back, only to be replaced again by the angels of being, and the two groups continued to alternate. When I woke up my mind sang, "do-be-do-be-do."

Can we manipulate dream imagery? Carl Jung certainly thought so. In effect, this would amount to knowing that you are dreaming while you're in the dream. In Eastern traditions the practice of cognition while dreaming is called dream yoga, which combines the creative potency of the dream state with diffuse ego-boundaries and conscious imagination. "Was it a vision, or a waking dream? Fled is that music: Do I wake or sleep?" wrote John Keats in his "Ode to a Nightingale."

Lucid dreaming, in which you are aware that you are dreaming, is the same state as practiced in dream yoga. In a way Friedrich August Kekule's snake dream that led to the discovery of the structure of the benzene molecule is an example of lucid dreaming. After his experience, Kekule became greatly enthusiastic about creative dreaming. "Let us learn to dream," he wrote.

Research suggests that how we participate in our dreams depends on our self-development. In particular, some researchers think that lucid dreaming may signal the beginning of a passage to higher states of conscious awareness. Neurophysiologist John Lilly used to advise "programming the biocomputer" before going to sleep; my own variation on this idea is asking your quantum consciousness to collapse in the form of a dream related to your quest, harnessing the power of intention.

Somewhere between alertness and sleep, brain waves change from the more commonplace and higher-frequency beta and alpha, to lower-frequency theta waves. There is some evidence that creativity may be enhanced when the brain produces theta waves. Physician Elmer Green had a breakthrough in his research while in a theta-wave-dominant drowsy state. Thomas Edison reportedly dozed in a comfortable chair with metal balls in his hands and two metal pans positioned below them on the floor. When Edison fell asleep the balls fell into the pans, creating a racket that would wake him so he could record his insights in the semistupor between sleep and waking.

Can drugs, especially psychedelic drugs, enhance creativity? Psychedelic drugs do lead us into altered states in which ego-boundaries are considerably enlarged; in that sense, they are similar to dream states. The difficulty in using such states for creativity is that creativity requires both heaven and earth, both the ego and nonlocal quantum modalities. Unfortunately, our ego functions seem to be disrupted by drug-induced altered states. And although there is no identifiable problem of dream addiction, there is such a problem with drugs; this, of course, is antithetical to finding freedom in the quantum modality, and its negative potential cannot be underestimated.

Working with Jungian Archetypes

Carl Jung emphasized the importance of working with some of the archetypes of the collective unconscious that seem particularly important to the way the unconscious drives of creativity express themselves. Jung's *anima* is the female archetype in men; it corresponds to the "female" experiences of thought and feeling. Jung's *animus* is the male archetype in women. Thanks to our conditioning, men tend to suppress anima, and women do much the same with their animus. But through unconscious processing each gender can access those suppressed qualities of the vital mind.

But why should we want to experience the vital energy and thought patterns of the other sex? A woman mystic in India, Meera

Bai, went to Brindaban, the birthplace of Krishna, a spiritual mecca of India, in search of a guru. But a venerable guru refused her because "she was a woman." She responded by saying, "I thought that in Brindaban everyone is a woman, that the only man is Krishna." The guru was very impressed with this reply, and its implication that we must all approach consciousness with the receptivity that is a core quality of the female experience. He accepted her as a disciple.

Jesus said in the *Gospel According to Thomas*, "When the male shall not be male, and the female not be female, then shall you enter [the kingdom of heaven]."

Another important Jungian archetype is the hero. In a sense, every creative act is the culmination of a hero's journey: The hero embarks on a quest, strives and endures, has insight, and then returns with the prize. In the *Iliad*, Zeus pulls all things to himself with a golden cord; similarly, the hero archetype attracts all of us. India has a different metaphor for the cord of inner creativity—the sound of Krishna's flute. But whether you have heard the flute or felt the tug of the cord, the result is the same; you set sail on an irreversible creative journey.

To integrate the hero, you must shun the ego and yield, during moments of intuition or insight, to the bidding of the archetype in your transformational journey. We see this vividly in the heroes and heroines of the *Iliad*, who are being manipulated by the gods (or archetypes) as if the characters were puppets.

The movie *The Accidental Tourist* offers a good depiction of a modern hero's journey. Macon Leary has lost touch with his anima. He shuns anything that is potentially painful, physical, or emotional, and thereby has abandoned creativity entirely. In order to return to the hero's journey, Macon has to be reinitiated. The job falls to a female, naturally: Muriel Pritchett, who brings in the energy of the East Indian goddess Kali, the cleanser of negativity. (Kali is a Bengali goddess worshipped in Calcutta. Nelson Mandela, when asked what he likes about Calcutta said, "This is the only city where they worship a black female god [Kali] standing on the body of a white male god [Siva].")

Macon makes a guarded start back toward life but, still reluctant to face pain, he returns to his wife when she beckons, even though the marriage doesn't work anymore. At the end Macon is running around searching for a taxi until he drops his baggage, both physically and symbolically. On his way to the airport he sees Muriel, who has followed him to Paris, and his dejected face gives way to a warm smile. Macon has broken through to his anima; he has rediscovered love.

All great creatives are heroes and heroines when they are functioning within the stages of a creative act.

Remembering Your dharma

Most of us get sidetracked by life; under pressure from family and society we give way to someone else's idea of how we should expend our life energy. Eventually many of us end up forgetting entirely what we came to this incarnation to achieve and to learn. Sooner or later we become unhappy, asking ourselves, what is the meaning of my life? When this happens in our forties and fifties, it is popularly known as a "midlife crisis."

The Sufi mystic Hafiz wrote, "Ever since Happiness heard your name it has been running through the streets trying to find you." I suggest a simple exercise for remembering your dharma. The trick is to realize that the moment you know what learnings you brought with you when you reincarnated this time, you will see your dharma with absolute clarity. The key is hidden in childhood memories that are no longer available through conscious recall.

Stage 1. Lie down comfortably on a mat on the floor. Do a body-awareness exercise: Breathe deeply a few times, then first become aware of your head, then your torso, your limbs, and finally, your whole body. Then recall a recent memory of an experience with a strong feeling and meaning tone. Visualize the characters in your memory experience vividly. Activate your chakras so the energies you feel now are the same as they were in your memory. Visualize the environment in as much detail as you can. Stay with this memory for a bit, and then let go.

This practice helps us get the hang of what an authentic memory recall feels like.

Stage 2. Begin with an intention exercise: Intend for quantum consciousness to evoke a childhood memory recall that will reveal your dharma. Promise to yourself that once you discover your dharma, you will follow it wherever it takes you. Assert that this intention of yours is for the greater good, attuned as it is with the evolutionary movement of consciousness. Gradually let the intention become a prayer. And end in silence for a minute or so.

Now choose a time in your childhood that you want to retrieve from your memory (anywhere between ages three and eight). Choose the most likely context for the incident you are trying to recall. Was there anyone else present? If so, produce them in your imagination. Now wait for your memory like a fisherman waits patiently with his baited hook. And like the fisherman, if you get a nibble, if a little bit of memory surfaces, coax the rest of the memory to come into view.

The entire exercise should take about half an hour. If you do this for a period of two weeks or so, you should expect some results. Once you know your dharma, and if it is not the path you are on, I encourage you to make the transition that your midlife crisis is asking you to make. Choose the path of your dharma, the path of your heart; synchronicity will support your choice. Stay in your dharma, think quantum, and be creative: Happiness will find you.

Oh mind, how slow you are to expand.
You cultivate one little field,
Fenced in by your ego.
Do you never face the horizon beyond?

As far as your consciousness reaches,
So can your husbandry,
Else the Great One, without your cultivation,
Remains barren, unconscious.

Oh mind, break open your fence, expand,
Cultivate, until, infinitely fertile,
Your field is lush with creativity.

CHAPTER 22

When Jane Meets Krishna: A Creative Encounter

The famous *Bhagavad Gita* is written as a dialog between the human Arjuna and Krishna, the "divine incarnate." It is a vivid depiction of the creative encounter between the ego and the quantum self—an encounter that lies at the heart of all creative acts. The following dialog respectfully (and playfully) borrows from the *Bhagavad Gita* to tell the story of an American woman who meets Krishna on the road to creativity.

Jane (puzzled and clearly disappointed): But you're not the author! I was hoping to ask the author some questions.

Krishna: I am Krishna. The author is busy, and has asked me to serve as his emissary.

Jane: Oh, okay. But I should warn you that I'm here to make a complaint. The flap copy persuaded me to read his book by promising to teach me creativity. But most of the researchers the author mentions say that successful creative people draw on a lot of traits that arise from factors like talent, creative upbringing, and genetics. Without those advantages, what can the rest of us do?

Krishna: Maybe you're interpreting the research too literally, not to mention pessimistically. You're seeing the glass half empty. What if I were to tell you that these traits you're aspiring to are mostly not causes but effects?

Jane (startled): What do you mean?

Krishna: Two creativity researchers followed a group of students from their art school days through the beginning of their adult careers. As a group they seemed to have the character traits that one associates with creative artists. And yet, when the researchers tracked down 31 of the students five or six years after they left art school, guess what? Only one had become a creative artist.

Jane: So what does that mean?

Krishna: Simply that the traits themselves are not the cause of creativity.

Jane: All right, forget traits. My father adhered to the dictum that children are to be seen and not heard. Although in my heart I knew better, and friends and teachers confirmed my own more positive view of myself, my father consistently intimidated and demeaned me. I guess I just don't have Michelangelo's ability to convert conflicts (in his case with the Pope) into great art! Anyway, Michelangelo was a creative genius and I'm not, even though I've learned a thing or two about creativity. Case closed.

Krishna: Don't be so fatalistic! What I am saying is this: Suppose Michelangelo developed this capacity for creativity because he realized that he *needed* it. He was hungry for creativity, but what he had instead was an unending conflict with an overbearing pope. So he worked with what he had, allowing the conflict to become fodder for unconscious processing, and converted it into wonderful art.

Jane: I don't understand.

Krishna: People are unwilling to hold conflicts close for fear that they may impair their ability to function in the world. So we rush to some superficial resolution. As F. Scott Fitzgerald said, "The test of first-rate intelligence is the ability to hold two opposite ideas in the mind at the same time and still retain the ability to function." But this is something you can develop through practice, as Michelangelo must have done.

Jane: You mean one of those "unity consciousness" experiences? I think that's reserved for mystic types, which I certainly am not.

Krishna: You probably had that experience as a child, but you've forgotten or suppressed it.

Jane: So you're agreeing with me: it was settled early on that I was not going to be a creative adult.

Krishna: Was it? What prevents you from discovering your connection with the subtle world even now?

Jane: I just don't think I can. So maybe my ego is the problem?

Krishna: But your ego is just an identity you put on, like clothes. If human beings were completely and irrevocably identified with their egos, no one would ever be creative.

Jane: Are you saying that someone like me can discover quantum reality at any age, even now?

Krishna: Yes, that's exactly what I'm saying. The real world is the subtle world, and it's yours! It's inside you. Give up your limiting self-image and discover your authentic self.

Jane: That's easy for you to say.

Krishna: But I am *your* quantum self. I'm not separate from you.

Jane: Oh, no? Then why am I so limited by my own conditioning, when you don't seem to have that problem?

Krishna: You're no more a slave to conditioning than I am. Creative people just choose not to be stymied by their negative conditioning. They go on being creative in spite of it. Why are you getting stuck in yours?

Jane: You're avoiding the issue. My question is this: Can anyone be creative? I say no. Maybe it just boils down to a matter of luck. But either way I don't see creativity in my future.

Krishna: Chance is not necessarily just luck, you know. They say that chance favors the prepared. And I agree with the author's belief that what seems to be chance may be synchronicity.

Jane: There it goes, my last chance at creativity.

Krishna: Jane, Jane. You insist on missing the message. You're enjoying your pessimism too much. Sure, creatives have many things going for them. But they don't start off with them; they develop them, they wake up to them.

Jane: But they have to begin somewhere. Where do I start?

Krishna: Most people begin by believing that creativity brings this and that—fame, attention, sex, money. So they get busy with situational creativity. But after a few lifetimes, they get bored and start to look at fundamental creativity: They become curious about whether major problems can really be solved. They start to investigate archetypes. They begin to pursue inner creativity.

Jane: Okay, I can see that. In my case, money, sex, and power aren't big motivations. And I do want to do something to make the world a better place. It sure seems like it could use some help.

Krishna (smiling): So what's stopping you?

Jane: I guess it's my own negativity.

Krishna: But I already told you that you can bypass negative emotions. Creativity can happen in spite of them.

Jane: Somehow that doesn't work for me. Call me a perfectionist.

Krishna: What do you think Jesus meant when he told his disciples, "Be ye as little children"?

Jane: Practice beginner's mind?

Krishna: Studies show that some of the same processes that people employ in their pursuit of inner creativity can help with outer creativity as well. For example, most practices of inner creativity slow you down, enabling you to "incubate" without getting antsy. This helps your outer creativity as well.

Jane: I do meditate, and I've noticed that my mind doesn't tend to race as much as it used to.

Krishna: There's more. If you watch your thoughts without attachment, defense, or interference, consciousness becomes relatively empty, receptive to *samadhi,* ready to resonate with the fundamental impulses of the universe.

Jane: Really?

Krishna: Really. Subhuti, a disciple of Buddha, was meditating under a tree when flowers began to shower down on him. "We are praising you for your discourse on emptiness of mind," a chorus of voices said. "But I haven't spoken," said Subhuti. "You haven't spoken, and we haven't heard. This is true emptiness," said the voices. And the petals continued to rain down.

When the mind becomes empty, when you transcend the ordinary mind of discourse, even for a moment, you become sensitive to the underlying creative reality. As you attune to the universe's purpose, your creative life blossoms.

Jane: I certainly have to admit that I feel inspired when I'm with you. But when I'm by myself, looking at the enormity of our problems, when I ponder all those countless millions of conservatives doing their best to maintain the status quo—or worse—I lose heart.

Krishna: So what else is new? Here's another story from India. Narada, the great celestial angel, was passing two mortals. One was a renunciate, who was meditating. He asked, "Oh, Narada, when shall I arrive?"

To this Narada said, "I have an appointment with God soon. I'll find out."

The second man was inhaling deeply from a hashish pipe, but he had the same question for Narada: "When shall I arrive?"

Narada laughed, but promised him also that he would ask God.

When Narada returned, he first went to the renunciate. "Well, what did God say? How many years longer need I meditate?"

"You have to meditate three more lifetimes," said Narada.

"Well, if nothing's going to happen in this lifetime, I may as well have some fun," said the renunciate, and he abandoned his practice.

The hashish smoker was also eager to hear from Narada.

"Well? What did God tell you?"

"See that tree over there? See all those leaves? That's how many lives it will take you to arrive," said Narada.

"Really? I'll arrive, too?" exclaimed the man, and he began dancing in ecstasy. And in that moment he arrived.

What do you think happened, Jane?

Jane: He really believed. So if I believe that I am creative right this very moment, I could break through?

Krishna: Not quite. He believed that God was on his side, after all. By the way, have you read my book?

Jane (startled): You have written a book?

Krishna: Well somebody transcribed my conversation with Arjuna, a meaning-seeker like you, and published it. I think it is still selling quite briskly. It is called the *Bhagavad Gita.*

Jane: I know about the *Bhagavad Gita,* but you can't possibly be *that* Krishna.

Krishna: The central message of the *Bhagavad Gita* is this: Whenever a mistaken worldview takes ascendancy, God comes to help those people who are willing to engage their creativity to right the wrong. In today's scientific language one would have to say the movement of consciousness will favor those who align themselves and their creativity with paradigm shifts, with purposive evolution.

Jane: In other words, if I do new paradigm work not only will it help me be creative (because what we need to create is simple stuff), but also the movement of consciousness will help me make a difference. How?

Krishna: Through synchronicity. The great psychologist Carl Jung correctly interpreted that the abundance of coincidences in the lives of creative people are not the result of mere chance but of divine cooperation.

Jane: Cool. Any other hints?

Krishna: Arjuna, the fellow I helped in the *Bhagavad Gita,* he, too, began suffering from anxiety neurosis like you when he saw the enormity of the battle that confronted him. I had to give him a big pep talk, but in retrospect I could have summarized all my teaching in two Sanskrit words: *Dharma* and *dharma.* They're actually the same word, but the first is spelled with a big *D* and the second with a little *d.*

Jane: I don't know Sanskrit. Please explain. What is big *D* Dharma?

Krishna: Big *D* Dharma is cosmic law, which includes the laws of evolution. As the story above illustrated, when you align yourself with Dharma, God is with you; the movement of consciousness supports you.

Jane: And what is the other dharma?

Krishna: The dharma with a little *d* is more subtle. We all come to this incarnation with a particular learning agenda. And we bring qualities from past incarnations that can help us fulfill that agenda.

Jane: That makes sense.

Krishna: Yes, but when opposition forces confront you, you will want to run like Arjuna, and you'll come up with impressive rationalizations to justify your actions. But don't run. Stay committed to your own dharma. Other people's dharma will get you into even bigger trouble.

Jane: Okay. You've convinced me. I'll remember to follow my dharma and align with Dharma.

Krishna: You have to do it of your own free will, not because I persuaded you.

Jane: But I don't have free will. I'm conditioned, remember?

Krishna: Wait a minute. You do have enough free will to say no. It's true that what you usually experience as free will, for example the decision to raise your arm, is not free. A neurophysiologist looking at an EEG connected to your brain will see electrical activity—called readiness potential—that will give away your intention fully 900 milliseconds ahead of your actual raising of the arm. But even after the readiness potential shows up, as soon as you become aware of your thought you can stop yourself from acting on it.

Jane (stunned): So when anxiety hits, I can stop that feeling. When fear tells me to run, I don't have to do it. . . .

Krishna: Exactly. Surrender your conflicts and anxieties. Say no to all the negative conditioning as long as you can. Don't be stymied by occasional failures. Practice so your *sattva*—your capacity for fundamental creativity—shines forth, and you can back that up with *rajas*—situational creativity—as needed. Awake, arise, and understand. Explore. Explore some more. Follow your dharma in the service of the creative universe's exploration of meaning and values, in the service of the evolutionary needs of humanity. Be committed to creativity and enter the process. Let the process transform you.

Jane: I can't wait.

> Ah! how wonderful creativity is,
> Savoring the joy of the world
> From our creative peaks.

Want the view permanently?

There is one little condition,
The world-joy-club membership fee.
We—you, too—must leap beyond the personal
To engage co-creatively with all.

Then we will all dance
To the music of harmonic creativity,
Together on our nonlocal dance floor.
Then reigns love—eternally.

ENDNOTES

Chapter 2

1. A. Goswami, *The Self-Aware Universe: How Consciousness Creates the Material World* (New York: Tarcher/Putnam, 1993) and A. Goswami, *God Is Not Dead: What Quantum Physics Tells Us about Our Origins and How We Should Live* (Charlottesville, VA: Hampton Roads, 2008).

Chapter 3

1. J. Grinberg-Zylberbaum, M. Delaflor, L. Attie, and A. Goswami, "The Einstein-Podolsky-Rosen Paradox in the Brain: The Transferred Potential," *Physics Essays* 7, no. 4 (December 1994): 422–28.

2. D. R. Hofstadter, *Gödel, Escher, Bach: An Eternal Golden Braid: A Metaphorical Fugue on Minds and Machines in the Spirit of Lewis Carroll* (New York: Basic Books, 1980).

3. R. Wagner, *My Life, Vol. 2* (London: Constable, 1911), 603.

Chapter 4

1. J. Arnold, "Creativity in Engineering," in *Creativity: An Examination of the Creative Process: A Report on the Third Communications Conference of the Art Directors Club of New York,* edited by P. Smith, 33–46 (New York: Hastings House, 1959).

Chapter 5

1. Quoted in K. Malville, *A Feather for Daedalus: Explorations in Science and Myth* (Menlo Park, CA: Cummings, 1975), 92–93.

2. H. Hesse, *Siddhartha* (London: Pan Books, 1973), 112.

3. K. Gibran, *The Prophet* (New York: Knopf, 1971), 75–76.

4. R. W. Weisberg, *Creativity: Beyond the Myth of Genius* (New York: Freeman, 1993).

Chapter 6

1. G. Wallas, *The Art of Thought* (New York: Harcourt, Brace, and World, 1926).

2. C. R. Rogers, "Toward a Theory of Creativity," in *Creativity and Its Cultivation: Addresses Presented at the Interdisciplinary Symposia on Creativity, Michigan State University, East Lansing, Michigan,* edited by H. H. Anderson, 69–82 (New York: Harper & Row, 1959).

Chapter 7

1. Quoted in J. Hadamard, *The Psychology of Invention in the Mathematical Field* (Princeton, NJ: Princeton University Press, 1939), 15.

2. Quoted in W. Harman and H. Rheingold, *Higher Creativity: Liberating the Unconscious for Breakthrough Insights* (New York: Tarcher, 1984), 35.

3. Ibid., 38–39.

4. Ibid., 46.

5. Ibid., 45.

6. A. Weil, *Health and Healing: From Herbal Remedies to Biotechnology, a Survey of Alternative Healing in the Search for Optimum Health* (New York: Houghton Mifflin, 1983).

7. D. Chopra, *Quantum Healing: Exploring the Frontiers of Mind/Body Medicine* (New York: Bantam-Doubleday, 1990) and A. Goswami, *The Quantum Doctor* (Charlottesville, VA: Hampton Roads, 2004).

8. A. Goswami, *Creative Evolution: A Physicist's Resolution between Darwinism and Intelligent Design* (Wheaton, IL: Theosophical Publishing House, 2008).

9. G. Bateson, *Mind and Nature: A Necessary Unity* (New York: Bantam, 1980), 336–337.

Chapter 8

1. D. Barrett, *The Committee of Sleep: How Artists, Scientists, and Athletes Use Dreams for Creative Problem-Solving—and How You Can Too* (New York: Crown, 2001).

2. C. G. Jung, *The Portable Jung*, edited by J. Campbell (New York: Viking, 1971).

3. N. Humphrey, "Seeing and Nothingness," *New Scientist* 53 (1972): 682–684.

4. A. J. Marcel, "Conscious and Preconscious Recognition of Polysemous Words: Locating the Selective Effect of Prior Verbal Context," in *Attention and Performance VIII*, edited by R. S. Nickerson, 435–458 (Hillsdale, NJ: Lawrence Erlbaum, 1980).

5. M. Sabom, *Recollections of Death: A Medical Investigation* (New York: Harper & Row, 1982).

6. K. Ring and S. Cooper, "Can the Blind Ever See? A Study of Apparent Vision During Near-Death and Out-of-Body Experiences." Preprint. (Storrs, CT: University of Connecticut, 1995).

Chapter 9

1. R. May, *The Courage to Create* (New York: W.W. Norton, 1994), 77.

2. B. Libet, E. W. Wright Jr., B. Feinstein, and D. Pearl, "Subjective Referral of the Timing for a Conscious Sensory Experience: A Functional Role for the Somatosensory Specific Projection System in Man," *Brain* 102 (1979): 193–224.

3. M. Csikszentmihalyi, *Flow: The Psychology of Optimal Experience* (New York: HarperCollins, 1990).

4. A. Goswami, "Creativity and the Quantum: A Unified Theory of Creativity," *Creativity Research Journal* 9, no. 1 (1996): 47–61.

5. B. Russell, *Portraits from Memory and Other Essays* (London: Allen and Unwin, 1965), 165.

6. R. N. Tagore, *Collected Poems and Plays* (London: Macmillan, 1913), 73.

7. Quoted in K. Malville, *A Feather for Daedalus*, 81–82.

8. W. Whitman, *The Poems of Walt Whitman (Leaves of Grass)* (New York: Thomas Y. Crowell Company, 1902), 165.

9. R. N. Tagore, *Later Poems of Rabindranath Tagore*, translated by A. Bose (New York: Minerva, 1976), 9.

Chapter 10

1. S. Freud, *Introductory Lectures on Psychoanalysis*, vol. XV of the Standard Edition (London: Hogarth, 1961) and S. Freud, *Introductory Lectures on Psychoanalysis*, vol. XVI of the Standard Edition (London: Hogarth, 1963).

2. J. Leyda and Z. Voynow, *Eisenstein at Work* (New York: Pantheon, 1982), ix.

3. J. Briggs, *Fire in the Crucible: The Self-Creation of Creativity and Genius* (Los Angeles: Tarcher, 1990).

4. C. G. Jung, "Approaching the Unconscious," in *Man and His Symbols,* edited by C. G. Jung. (New York: Dell, 1971).

5. C. G. Jung and W. Pauli. *The Interpretation of Nature and the Psyche* (New York: Pantheon, 1955).

Chapter 11

1. P. Brook, *The Shifting Point: 1946–1987* (London: Methuen Drama, 1988), 114.

2. A. Goswami, *Creative Evolution.*

3. R. N. Tagore, *The Religion of Man* (New York: MacMillan, 1931), 93.

4. Quoted in J. Briggs, *Fire in the Crucible,* 36.

5. W. Wordsworth, *The Prelude, 1799, 1805, 1850,* edited by J. Wordsworth, M. Abrams, and S. Gill (New York: Norton, 1979).

Chapter 12

1. J. P. Guilford, "Traits of Creativity," in *Creativity and Its Cultivation: Addresses Presented at the Interdisciplinary Symposia on Creativity, Michigan State University, East Lansing, Michigan,* edited by H. H. Anderson, 142–161 (New York: Harper & Row, 1959) and E. P. Torrance, "The Nature of Creativity as Manifest in its Testing," in *The Nature of Creativity: Contemporary Psychological Perspectives,* edited by R. J. Sternberg, 43–75 (Cambridge, U.K.: Cambridge University Press, 1988).

2. E. De Bono, *Lateral Thinking: Creativity Step by Step* (New York: Harper & Row, 1970).

3. D. W. Mackinnon, "The Personality Correlates of Creativity: A Study of American Architects," in *Proceedings of the Fourteenth International Congress*

of Applied Psychology, Volume 2, edited by G. S. Nielsen, 11–39 (Copenhagen: Munskgaard, 1962).

Chapter 13

1.   A. Goswami, *Physics of the Soul: The Quantum Book of Living, Dying, Reincarnation, and Immortality* (Charlottesville, VA: Hampton Roads, 2001).

2.   I. Stevenson, *Children Who Remember Previous Lives: A Question of Reincarnation* (Charlottesville: University Press of Virginia, 1987).

3.   For a discussion read J. Briggs, *Fire in the Crucible,* 253–258.

Chapter 14

1.   I. Rabi, "Profiles—Physicists, I." *The New Yorker Magazine* (October 13, 1975), 108.

2.   W. Harman and C. de Quincey, *The Scientific Exploration of Consciousness: Toward an Adequate Epistemology.* Research Report. (Sausalito, CA: Institute of Noetic Sciences, 1994).

Chapter 15

1.   J. W. Aldridge, *Talents and Technicians: Literary Chic and the New Assembly-Line Fiction* (New York: Macmillan, 1992), 25.

2.   D. H. Lawrence, *A Selection from Phoenix* (London: Penguin Books, 1971), 430.

Chapter 16

1.   M. Ray and R. Myers, *Creativity in Business* (New York: Doubleday, 1989), 144–145.

2.   A. Goswami, "Conscious Economics," in *Aspects of Consciousness: Essays on Physics, Death and the Mind,* edited by I. Fredriksson, 178–203 (Jefferson, N.C.: McFarland, 2012).

Chapter 17

1. A. Goswami, *How Quantum Activism Can Save Civilization: A Few People Can Change Human Evolution* (Charlottesville, VA: Hampton Roads, 2011).

2. Adapted by Amit Goswami.

Chapter 18

1. Rumi, *These Branching Moments,* translated by J. Moyne and C. Barks (Providence, Rhode Island: Copper Beech Press, 1988), 2.

Chapter 19

1. R. N. Tagore, *Later Poems of Rabindranath Tagore*, 3.

2. F. Merrell-Wolff, *The Philosophy of Consciousness Without an Object: Reflections on the Nature of Transcendental Consciousness* (New York: Julian Press, 1973), 38–55.

Chapter 20

1. S. Sivananda, *Vedanta (Jnana Yoga)* (Rishikesh, India: Divine Life Society, 1987).

INDEX

ABOUT THE AUTHOR

Amit Goswami, Ph. D., is a retired professor from the theoretical physics department of the University of Oregon in Eugene, where he had served since 1968. He is a pioneer of the new paradigm known as "science within consciousness."

Goswami is the author of the highly successful textbook *Quantum Mechanics,* which is used in universities throughout the world. He has also written many popular books, including *The Self-Aware Universe, The Visionary Window, Physics of the Soul, The Quantum Doctor,* and *God Is Not Dead.*

Goswami appeared in the films *What the Bleep Do We Know?* and *The Dalai Lama Renaissance,* and the award-winning documentary *The Quantum Activist.* Learn more at www.amitgoswami.org.

Hay House Titles of Related Interest

YOU CAN HEAL YOUR LIFE, the movie, starring Louise Hay & Friends
(available as a 1-DVD program and an expanded 2-DVD set)
Watch the trailer at: www.LouiseHayMovie.com

THE SHIFT, the movie,
starring Dr. Wayne W. Dyer
(available as a 1-DVD program and an expanded 2-DVD set)
Watch the trailer at: www.DyerMovie.com

•••

THE BIOLOGY OF BELIEF: Unleashing the Power of Consciousness, Matter &
Miracles, by Bruce H. Lipton, Ph.D.

DEEP TRUTH: Igniting the Memory of Our Origin, History, Destiny, and Fate,
by Gregg Braden

E-SQUARED: Nine Do-It-Yourself Energy Experiments that Prove Your
Thoughts Create Your Reality, by Pam Grout

ONE MIND: How Our Individual Mind Is Part of a Greater Consciousness
and Why It Matters, by Larry Dossey, M.D.

All of the above are available at your local bookstore,
or may be ordered by contacting Hay House (see next page).

•••

We hope you enjoyed this Hay House book. If you'd like to receive our online catalog featuring additional information on Hay House books and products, or if you'd like to find out more about the Hay Foundation, please contact:

Hay House, Inc., P.O. Box 5100, Carlsbad, CA 92018-5100
(760) 431-7695 or (800) 654-5126
(760) 431-6948 (fax) or (800) 650-5115 (fax)
www.hayhouse.com® • www.hayfoundation.org

———

Published in Australia by: Hay House Australia Pty. Ltd.,
18/36 Ralph St., Alexandria NSW 2015
Phone: 612-9669-4299 • *Fax:* 612-9669-4144
www.hayhouse.com.au

Published in the United Kingdom by: Hay House UK, Ltd.,
The Sixth Floor, Watson House, 54 Baker Street, London W1U 7BU
Phone: +44 (0)20 3927 7290 • *Fax:* +44 (0)20 3927 7291
www.hayhouse.co.uk

Published in India by: Hay House Publishers India,
Muskaan Complex, Plot No. 3, B-2, Vasant Kunj, New Delhi 110 070
Phone: 91-11-4176-1620 • *Fax:* 91-11-4176-1630
www.hayhouse.co.in

———

Access New Knowledge.
Anytime. Anywhere.

Learn and evolve at your own pace
with the world's leading experts.

www.hayhouseU.com

Printed in the United States
By Bookmasters